PARISH PRIEST

PARISH PRIEST

Father Michael McGivney and American Catholicism

DOUGLAS BRINKLEY
AND JULIE M. FENSTER

wm
WILLIAM MORROW
An Imprint of HarperCollins*Publishers*

HarperCollins books may be purchased for educational, business, or sales promotional use. For information please write: Special Markets Department, HarperCollins Publishers, 10 East 53rd Street, New York, NY 10022.

FIRST EDITION

Designed by Sarah Maya Gubkin

Printed on acid-free paper

Library of Congress Cataloging-in-Publication Data

Brinkley, Douglas.
    Parish priest : Father Michael McGivney and American Catholicism / Douglas Brinkley and Julie M. Fenster.—1st ed.
      p. cm.
    Includes bibliographical references (p.).
    ISBN-13: 978-0-06-077684-8
    ISBN-10: 0-06-077684-6
    1. McGivney, Michael J. (Michael Joseph), 1852–1890. 2. Catholic Church—United States—Clergy—Biography. 3. Priests—United States—Biography. 4. Knights of Columbus—Biography. I. Fenster, J. M. (Julie M.) II. Title.

BX4705.M194B75   2006
282'.092—dc22
[B]
                                 2005044382

06   07   08   09   10   WBC/RRD   10 9 8 7 6 5 4 3

For *Reverend Gabriel O'Donnell, O.P.*

And for two parish priests,
Father Charles Borgononi,
Diocese of Syracuse, New York
AND
Father James Carter,
Diocese of New Orleans, Louisiana

Contents

Preface: The Same Manner to All Human Souls

He was a man of the people. He was zealous of the people's welfare, and all the kindliness of his priestly soul asserted itself more strongly in his unceasing efforts for the betterment of their condition.

—Description of Father Michael McGivney, read at his first memorial service (1890)

In 1998, when we were working together on a book for *American Heritage,* we took a break from a meeting and noticed an article in *The New York Times* about an obscure—to us, at least—priest from Connecticut who was under consideration for sainthood. Written by Frances Chamberlain and titled "Was There a Saint Born in Waterbury?" the piece described the life of Michael McGivney (1852–1890) and acknowledged that he met the general criteria for canonization.[1]

That *New York Times* article couldn't have come along at a more fortuitous time for us. In the course of our discussions for the *American Heritage* book, *The History of the United States,* we marveled at the transition of Catholics in this country, from reviled victims of Know-Nothing violence in the mid-nineteenth century to respected members of mainstream America only a few generations later. Father McGivney's life spanned that era in U.S. history and even helped lead the successful search for a Catholic sense of belonging, through his creation of the fraternal group, the Knights of Columbus, in 1882.

At the same time, the McGivney article reopened a continuing conversation we'd been having on the subject of the priesthood. We had both long been intrigued with the ideal and the reality of priestly life. Historically, priests represent a continuum of centuries, if not millennia. Other professions, or callings, are characterized by the ways in which they change with the times: the medical doctors of today would bedazzle their predecessors. The postmodern artists—well, they might perplex the masters of old. But priests are characterized most by those ways in which they have changed the least.

Father Michael McGivney seemed to meld these two seemingly disparate fascinations on our part. He was a priest—that historical constant—who lived in the midst of great change and even fomented some part of it. Intellectually, that is what drew us to learn more about Father McGivney, a compelling figure. Compassionate and lamblike by nature, he had to develop a tougher side, too, in order to fulfill his obligations as a priest. We were both delighted to find that he loved the sport of baseball his whole adult life. We couldn't help but respect his unshakable faith in God. Although we are not theologians, we continued to delve into the life of

Michael McGivney for the light it shed on his times and his calling.

Only a little later, in 2002, a year rocked by scandals revolving around child molestations perpetrated by Roman Catholic priests, we began to recognize that we felt personally conflicted. Like many others, we each counted at least a few priests among the most impressive people we had ever known. The idea of taking a new look at the priesthood in America through one of its most exemplary representatives was, the more we spoke about it, not merely intriguing but imperative. We decided to write a book about Father McGivney—on one hand, the man who had founded the largest Catholic men's fraternal organization in the world, and on the other, just as important, the most unassuming of Catholic clerics.

In other words, we decided to write a McGivney biography largely because he was "just a parish priest." Too often American Catholic history focuses on the Church hierarchy, much as general history focuses too often on royalty and presidents. Over the years, grand biographies have been written about famous bishops and cardinals. That's fine, but the heart of Catholicism in the United States lies with the parish priests, who become so much a part of their parishioners' regular lives. They celebrate Mass, baptize infants, visit the sick and dying, and preside at weddings and funerals. It's the parish priest to whom many of America's 65 million Catholics turn in times of personal crisis or if poverty strikes a family. They serve on the level of one human helping another. By writing about Father McGivney, we're embracing that very obscurity and so honoring *all* parish priests—or, more than that, seeking to understand

their calling just a little bit more clearly. Too often, their sto-
ries, if they are told at all, are buried in parish newsletters and
local newspapers. Worse, due to those who are guilty of un-
conscionable crimes, parish priests in general have been
smeared in the popular imagination. We hope an account of
McGivney's life will help to instigate fresh thinking on the
priesthood and its manifest potential.

Taking on a serious biography of a parish priest was fraught
with obstacles. Few of Father McGivney's letters have survived and he didn't keep a diary. He died when he was only
thirty-eight years old. The paper trail was thin. But there was
some encouraging news. The Knights of Columbus—
headquartered in New Haven, just blocks from Yale
University—kept detailed records on the early years of their
organization. For years, the order has sought material related
to Father McGivney, a process that has, if anything, gained
momentum in recent years. Because Father McGivney is being considered for sainthood, Father Gabriel O'Donnell, postulator of his cause, has traveled widely in search of source
material on the life of Michael McGivney. While all of this
primary and secondary source material was useful, we found
McGivney's church records, in particular, extremely important in recounting the life and times of the hardworking
priest. The bulk of the research, however, came with our pe-
rusal of every available local periodical for the span 1878 to
1890, McGivney's working years. The final list included fourteen papers, most notably the *New Haven Union* and the *Connecticut Catholic*. We found these many periodicals at Yale

University's Sterling Memorial Library and at the Connecticut Historical Society in Hartford. Court records and other contemporary material filled in other gaps.

Calm, mild-mannered, and dutiful, Father McGivney was known in Catholic circles around New England as a pure-hearted reformer. There was, by all accounts, something both stoic and angelic about his nature. One of his goals was the promulgation of insurance for Catholics in the working classes. With that as a primary motivation, the Knights of Columbus was founded. Ever since Father McGivney created the group in the basement of St. Mary's Church on Hillhouse Avenue in New Haven, the Knights of Columbus have flourished.

Only time will tell whether Father McGivney becomes the first American parish priest to achieve sainthood. His cause has already fulfilled some of the requirements. McGivney has been deceased for over five years, of course, and is the cause of popular devotions. "A miracle is necessary in order to achieve beatification—and the advocates of Father McGivney's cause could wait decades for that to happen," Frances Chamberlain wrote in the *New York Times*. "However, there have already been some claims of miracles which are being investigated. . . . Canonization, the next step, is recognition that this person is in heaven and can be called a saint. Another miracle is essential to move from beatification to canonization. Once the miracle is investigated and found to be true, the Pope . . . can declare that person a saint."

It is not our purpose as historians to weigh in on whether Father Michael J. McGivney deserves sainthood. That is best left in the hands of the Roman Catholic Church. What we do know, however, is that McGivney has a place even beyond Catholic history. The day is not far off when books of general American history will carry his name in the index, with space devoted to his influence over the development of American values and character. A biography of this Connecticut man, this parish priest, has been long overdue.

Douglas Brinkley
New Orleans, Louisiana

Julie M. Fenster
DeWitt, New York

PARISH PRIEST

1

A FRIEND OF THE FAMILY

Not that the state of Connecticut had anything against Catholics in the early 1800s—but they weren't allowed to purchase land. If the issue was pressed, then special dispensation might be granted, but only through an act of the legislature. All the while, Catholics were expected to join with most of the rest of the populace in paying a tax for the support of the Congregational Church, the state's official religion at the time.[1] Episcopals, Baptists, and Quakers were all exempted, but not Catholics. It was no wonder that Connecticut, with almost 300,000 residents, counted its Catholic population in the dozens. Yet none of that stopped Michael and Bridget Downes from moving there.

Their previous homeland was far worse for Catholics, and little better for Protestants. Ireland in the early nineteenth century was a land of enforced poverty, where few farmers owned their own acreage and the landlords, most of them living in England or on the European continent, choked out all hope of improvement by charging unreasonably high rents. *The Times* of London, a conservative newspaper that traditionally spared little sympathy for the Irish, sent a correspondent to County Donegal and received a description of a typical rural landscape: "From one end of [the landlord's] estate here to the other nothing is to be found but poverty, misery, wretched cultivation and infinite subdivision of land. There are no gentry, no middle class, all are poor, wretchedly poor. Every shilling the tenants can raise from their half-cultivated land is paid in rent, whilst the people subsist for the most part on potatoes and water."[2]

Even before the potato blight of 1845 led to the Great Famine, alert Irishmen were facing such facts and the sad impossibility of being Irish. "The conviction that the country held no future existed as early as 1815," William Forbes Adams wrote in his classic history *Ireland and Irish Emigration to the New World*.[3] The Downes family escaped early on, sailing for America with their young son in 1827.[4] Their specific destination was the state of Connecticut, where a few of their old neighbors had settled already.

For more than a dozen years, Michael Downes, known as Mikey, was a common laborer, probably finding work building canals or railroads, as did most of his countrymen. In 1832, he and Bridget moved to New Haven. By no coincidence, the city's first Roman Catholic congregation was established there the same year, serving about three hundred people. It would be in keeping with the devout Downes family to settle within the embrace of a parish, once that option was available.

In another respect, too, New Haven was ripe territory for people such as the Downeses. Mikey and Bridget were dedicated to reading and education. New Haven, a manufacturing town and an active port, was influenced most of all by Yale University. Founded in 1701 as a rather rigid Puritan institution, Yale would loosen up considerably in the nineteenth century, combining high academic standards with a rebellious spirit. The campus took up one whole side of the flat, grassy Green that formed the hub of New Haven life. Rising tall, like a citadel in fieldstone, Yale took little notice of New Haven's latest family of Irish immigrants. The Downeses were just a working-class couple trailing three young sons, William, Edward, and John, as they walked along the Green and looked up at the great university.

Mikey Downes started work in New Haven as a news hawk, selling one New Haven paper or another on the street. The work suited him and a short time later he was a full-time newsdealer—said to be the city's very first—stocking an array of New Haven and New York papers in a corner kiosk.[5] It was a major accomplishment for him at the time, but he wasn't through. Like most of his countrymen, disenchanted with farming as they had known it in Ireland, he regarded storekeeping as the province of truly unlimited opportunity.

Only about 1 percent of first-generation Irish immigrants managed to fulfill the dream of opening a shop;[6] Downes joined their ranks in the early 1840s, when he rented a space at the prime corner of Church and Chapel streets, on the Green looking diagonally across to Yale. Customers could buy papers or, for two cents, go in the back room and read as many of the New York papers as they wanted. Political debates with the proprietor were free of charge.

Mikey and Bridget also owned property—although by the time they bought a wood-frame house in 1843, the state legislature didn't have to know about it. The law requiring special dispensation for land ownership by Catholics had been lifted ten years before. The days of official antagonism toward Catholics were over. Unofficial anti-Catholic fervor was surging to new peaks, though. To combat the image of immigrant Catholics, especially Irish ones, as disloyal and shiftless, the Downes family was intent on showing that they belonged in America.

In 1845, with the store making the Downes name famous in New Haven, Mikey died suddenly. His second son Edward, only sixteen, took over the family store. With his help, and the encouragement of Bridget, the youngest of the three Downes boys, John, graduated from Yale Medical School in 1854. Immediately popular in his practice, he died of tuberculosis at the age of just twenty-six. The oldest son, William, later graduated from Yale Law School. Extremely successful in his own right, he was pointed out as "New Haven's only Catholic lawyer" until his own early death, also from tuberculosis.

Through the years, the store was left entirely to Edward, who continually expanded his small empire until, in the late 1860s, it was "Edward Downes, Stationer and Newsdealer, at Wholesale and Retail."[7] From art supplies to comic magazines, he sold anything pertaining to paper goods and watched over one of New Haven's most thriving businesses. Edward Downes also presided over a family that would eventually include six children born to his first wife, two to his second, and six more to his third wife, Catherine. On Sunday mornings in the years before the youngest was born, fourteen of the fifteen members of the Downes family could be seen filing into St. Mary's Church on Hillhouse Avenue. The fifteenth, Josephine, would already be there; she was the church organist.

Like any Catholic church, St. Mary's attracted all kinds of people, but in New Haven, it had something of a corner on the energetic and ambitious set. In part, that may have been a result of its setting: an imposing stone structure, almost like an unofficial cathedral for the city, it sat on Hillhouse Avenue, New Haven's most prestigious street. For all of its timeless stonework and hints of English Gothic architecture, St. Mary's was the newest Catholic church in town, dedicated in 1874. By then, New Haven counted five parishes, but none was quite like St. Mary's. The building itself satisfied something deep within local Catholic leaders like Edward Downes, but for those in his children's generation, there was an even more appealing glow. They knew that inside, they had a friend, which is the quality that makes any church come to life.

In Father Michael McGivney, the youthful parishioners of St. Mary's looked to a priest who could be one of them, not merely because he loved a good laugh as much as anyone else or a snappy play in baseball even more, but because he knew what it was to be "first generation" or "second generation." He knew what it was to look for and find a place as both an American and a Roman Catholic. All of his parishioners were trying to do that same thing, along one course or another. Some, like Josephine Downes, would eventually follow him into a life in the Church. Others wanted to move forward amid the fast pace of life in America without falling out of step with the daily relevance of their religion. In either case, Father McGivney's strong belief lay with the strength of the family. He was fascinated by the power derived there—not through need, but on the contrary, through being needed. The parents for each other and for the children, the children for one another and for the parents, too: obligations fulfilled. Therein lay the potential in aspects practical and spiritual. That was McGivney's philosophy and it was already absolute within him when he was only in his twenties. Fortunately, his personal style was not nearly so staunch. Marked by laughter and empathy, his charm lay in the ability to align himself with people of any age group.

As Father McGivney came to know each of the Downeses—a process that admittedly took some time—he formed a particular friendship with Edward Downes Jr., the stationer's son, who was also planning to serve the Church. A natural scholar, Edward Jr. was a student at St. Charles College near Ellicott City, Maryland, which he entered in 1876 at the age of sixteen. According to the school catalogue, St. Charles's only object was to educate "Catholic youths who aspire to the holy priesthood."[8] Housed in a single, expansive building in the middle of the Maryland countryside, it was an independent institution, but one generally regarded as a prep school for St. Mary's University and Theological Seminary of St. Sulpice, which was located in Baltimore. None of this was foreign to Father McGivney; he had received his own education at St. Mary's Seminary.

St. Charles described itself as "strictly a preparatory ecclesiastical seminary," with the emphasis, it seems, on the word "strictly." The permission of the president was necessary for a student to correspond with anyone except his parents and pastor. That was not all. "To guard against the loss of time and danger to morals, incident to the reading of frivolous or bad books,"[9] the boys weren't allowed to read anything except material assigned by their professors. For a fellow like Edward Downes Jr., who had grown up surrounded by frivolous books (and no doubt more than a few bad ones among them), such constraints might have seemed downright unnatural—or, on the other hand, a welcome relief. However he felt about that rule, one thing is certain: he thrived in the atmosphere of St. Charles. In the spring of 1881, he graduated as salutatorian of his class.[10] At twenty-one, he was ready to pursue his long-standing dream of entering the priesthood, making plans to enter St. Mary's Seminary that fall. His younger brother Alfred, at eighteen, had plans, too; he was headed for Yale Law School.

For years, Edward Downes Sr. and his brood were regarded as "the oldest, richest and most respected Catholic family of New Haven."[11] Over most of those years, it was true enough, yet by 1881, anyone who was still saying it was just being kind. Or else they didn't know the truth.

Edward Sr. had been caught off guard by the Panic of 1873, an economic downturn that stubbornly outlasted his ability to keep up with his creditors. Eventually, he lost the store, along with his portfolio of investments, mostly in the form of real estate. The family moved into a succession of smaller houses, until they were back in the Howe Street home in which Edward had grown up; it was not really large enough for his flock, but somehow they squeezed in. And somehow, Edward managed to keep up appearances in the business community. Before long, he had a new store in a downtown location, selling news and paper goods. He still had more debts than assets, though, unless one counted the family that, through it all, he managed to keep around him. He and Catherine were even expecting a new baby as 1881 drew to a close.

Edward Sr. had hope that he could rebuild his fortune, and at fifty-two, he had plenty of time, or so it seemed as he bustled off to his strangely smaller, quieter newsstand every day. Edward Sr. would not live to see out the year, though, dying of "brain fever" in late December. That may have been the coroner's generalized term for malaria, or perhaps it was simply a way of saying that the disappointments of business had been deeper than Edward Sr. ever let on.

The Downeses had built their position, along with their wealth, over the course of almost fifty years after Michael and Bridget Downes arrived in New Haven in 1832.[12] It only took a single day for it all to unravel. With the death of Edward Sr., the extent of the Downeses' financial reversal became a matter of public record. But that was not the worst of it.

The hold that Edward had somehow been able to maintain on a bright future for his children collapsed, as the court loomed ready to take charge of their fates. Even that was not the worst of it, though. The final tragedy was that Edward's widow, Catherine, didn't know where to turn for help.

Edward Sr. didn't leave any money. In the winter of 1882, Catherine slowly tried to get over grieving for her husband—but the weight of all that confronted her family was even more overwhelming. As each day dawned, she had to face the fact that she didn't know who would provide for her children and stepchildren, and save the future for them. In fact, the County of New Haven in its official capacity wondered the same thing. When a family had no source of income, the Probate Court had the right to assign the children to public institutions. Although the law cast the ugly specter of breaking up families, it was actually in place to protect children from possible neglect. It was also meant to spare the community from the delinquency of ill-supervised teenagers. The Probate Court demanded proof from families like the Downeses that children left fatherless would not become vagrants. Catherine Downes was unable to provide that assurance.

Edward Jr. had no choice but to quit the seminary. He returned home to run the news counter.

During January, Edward Jr. made a convincing case that, young as he was, he could manage the store and provide for his widowed stepmother and the youngest of the children. The court turned its attention to the three teenaged boys: Alfred, nineteen; George, seventeen; and Joseph, fourteen. With no money available for education or apprenticeships, the judge ruled that guardians had to be found for each of them or else the court would intervene. The guardian had to be a person of good character, someone acceptable to the court. There were plenty of people who fit that description in the upstanding city of New Haven, most of them old friends of Edward Downes Sr. The guardian had to take full responsibility for the actions and well-being of the ward. That narrowed the list of volunteers considerably, even in regard to the well-reared Downes teenagers. A teenager could be a volatile entity in any era and in any family.

Finally, the guardian had to put up a bond of more than

$1000. That pretty well emptied the list of potential guardians for the Downes teens, although relatives eventually banded together in order to vouch for the two younger ones, George and Joseph. On February 2, 1882, New Haven's Probate Court accepted $2500 for each of them in the form of a bond from their new guardians. That left Alfred. The court set a price of $1500 on the privilege of becoming his guardian. His hearing was set for February 6.

For all of the powerful connections that the Downeses had in New Haven, in business circles, in politics, and in the leadership of the local Irish-American community, no one came forward. Edward Sr.'s many old friends disappeared, claiming that either they didn't have time or they hadn't the money to spare.

On the sixth, a Monday, people all over New Haven were complaining. They were also digging out, after winter storms over the weekend had made a particularly messy job of leaving a foot of snow on the ground. The trains were backed up, and even the steamboats taking passengers back and forth to New York City were running late.[13] More to the point for New Haven residents with business downtown, the sidewalks were still piled with snow, as landlords, running late, too, neglected to shovel their sections.[14]

Only the New Haven Probate Court was running on time. Edward Jr. was there, in place of Catherine, who was in confinement, expecting her baby within two months. His younger brother Alfred answered a series of questions posed by the judge. Then the judge asked the court if anyone was present to enter into a guardianship for Alfred Downes. Alfred looked back at the gallery.

Michael McGivney stood up, a slightly built man with a

smooth complexion made rosy by the brisk winter air. For some of the older people present, it was a surprise even to see a Catholic priest in a government building. Until Father McGivney's generation, priests tended to remain on church property as much as possible, in emphasis of the greater glories to be found there. By the bustling 1880s, as the situation became less proscribed, priests did venture out regularly, whether or not they were on church business. Nonetheless, even the most worldly among them stopped short of actually seeking out a role in any other institution.

For Father McGivney, however, the New Haven Probate Court was exactly the right place for a parish priest on that February morning. A family was at stake. And so, when the judge asked whether anyone present would act as guardian for Alfred Downes, McGivney rose to his feet. If others in the court turned to stare at the youthful priest in his long black cassock, that couldn't be helped. McGivney was no revolutionary, enjoying change for its own sake. Quite the opposite, in fact. But he was a man of action, born with an unresting sense of compassion, embraced by an entirely practical turn of mind.

Father McGivney didn't have $1500 for the bond, but he did have the trust of a retired grocer named Patrick McKiernan. With the judge's approval, McKiernan acted as surety, guaranteeing that if Father McGivney reneged on the guardianship, he would pay the "penal sum" of $1500. A bond was signed to that effect.[15] Alfred had a guardian who believed in his future, in place of his late father.

Father McGivney left the Probate Court well satisfied at the outcome of the Downes case, but not at the prevalence of the same problem throughout the community and even the nation. Even though he was only a young man, he was filled with a lifetime of anger and frustration at the sense of doom that settled over nearly every family that lost its wage earner. Long before, he had watched firsthand, when it fell over his own family. On the afternoon of February 6, he was more determined than ever that what had happened to the Downes family need not happen to anyone else.

As Father McGivney walked home across the Green, dodging the snowdrifts along with everyone else, he prepared in his mind for a crucial meeting that evening at St. Mary's, a meeting that would extend the sense of family within the laity of the Catholic Church. It would be a turning point, if he could carry his point with the men invited to be there. All of them were Catholics and most were men of action, ambitious for success. If they weren't rich yet, they would be quick to point out that they also weren't finished trying, just yet. In any case, they were busy men, which meant that they could get things done, if they wanted to badly enough. Of course, it also meant that they could say no in a dozen different ways or—even more ominously—say "maybe" in just one. Father McGivney knew all of that. But it was the echoing uncertainty of the afternoon session in Probate Court that made him walk a little faster.

The special strengths of Catholicism could be planted in men, he thought, especially husbands and fathers, to grow with them through their lives. And beyond, as well, with widows having a place to turn and children keeping hold of the future that their fathers intended. Michael McGivney had an understanding of them all: the fathers, the mothers, the children, an everyday trinity more fragile in modern life than anyone else seemed to realize.

2

AN AMERICAN CHILD

Michael McGivney was raised in Waterbury, Connecticut, about twenty-five miles northwest of New Haven along the Naugatuck River. By the time he was born in 1852, Waterbury was already known as the Brass City for its steaming forges, and it was fast heading toward its later title of the Most Catholic City in America.[1]

Connecticut, the home of inventors and industrialists, set the pace for American manufacturing in the mid-nineteenth century. Burgeoning communities, especially in the southwestern part of the state, created new jobs by the thousands. It did not take much more than that to draw immigrants, many of whom were Catholic. Both aspects of Waterbury, its industry and growing church, were attractions for Michael's father, Patrick McGivney, who arrived in America at the age of twenty-four in 1849, with that great influx of immigrants forced out of Ireland by famine and unrest.

Mary Lynch was part of the same wave in 1849, and like Patrick, she sprang from County Cavan in the Irish midland, although the two were from different towns and there is no reason to think that they were acquainted before settling in Waterbury. Mary was only fifteen when she arrived, nine years younger than Patrick.[2] Yet one year later, at sixteen, she was a bride, wedded to Patrick McGivney in St. Peter's Church, Waterbury.[3] Both families had once been modestly prosperous in Ireland. Any of the relatives at the wedding supper could linger around the table and boast of decent farms back home or of ancestors important in the Church there. But in America, that was nothing but talk. In America, Patrick and Mary had to start all over. The famine had knocked them out of Ireland, but at least they were still alive.

Patrick McGivney had arrived in America without a trade. Under the same circumstances, most of his countrymen resorted to unskilled labor. McGivney, however, soon learned iron molding, creating the casts into which molten metal was poured to make machine parts or other objects. It was a good job, demanding concentration and finesse, but not every last bit of a man's strength. And a molder received good wages, enough to keep his family well fed and in an attractive house. The same wasn't always true of day laborers, who exhausted themselves digging dirt or hauling cargo and still lived in a state of poverty. Inside a foundry, however, the one thing that a molder never received was clean, fresh air.

In 1852, Patrick McGivney was working for a man named

Merrit Nichols, an entrepreneur who had not only a brass factory but affordable houses to rent. One was a cottage on the Naugatuck River's west bank, an area that was almost entirely undeveloped at the time. The McGivneys reveled in it. To reach the foundry, Patrick crossed the railroad tracks that ran alongside the river. Then he walked across a wire bridge that led over the water into Waterbury proper. He undoubtedly looked forward to the return trip every night. Forty-eight years later, a veteran reporter wrote of the McGivney place:

> In those days it was a romantic spot and the few Irish people who lived [in Waterbury] at that time considered it a rare treat to call upon Mr. McGivney and his wife and spend an afternoon in their companionship beneath the shade of the dense foliage that surrounded the cottage, where the music of the river, the song of myriads of wild birds and an occasional shriek from a locomotive were the only things that broke the stillness of their rural home.[4]

On August 12, 1852, two years after the McGivneys were married, Mary gave birth to her first child, Michael Joseph, in the quaint cottage on the riverbank. Michael J. McGivney was baptized on August 19 by the Reverend Michael O'Neile, the burly priest who had brought the Catholic Church to Waterbury only a few years before.

Not long after arriving from Ireland himself, Father O'Neile had been assigned by the bishop of the Hartford Diocese, Bernard O'Reilly (another native Irishman), to serve as the Naugatuck Valley's first resident pastor. Father O'Neile initially tried to start a church in the town of Derby, but without success.[5] In 1847, Father O'Neile moved in with a sympathetic family in Waterbury and managed to open St. Peter's Church in a building he purchased for $550 from the local Episcopal parish. The only stipulation was that the structure had to be moved from its original site. That didn't stop Michael O'Neile or the people around him, who longed for a community of worship. The total price of St. Peter's, counting the move and the "cost of ground" as Father O'Neile put it, was $2290.[6] With Father O'Neile's energy and the rapid expansion of his parish, the debt was repaid as of September 1, 1852, only a few weeks after Michael Joseph McGivney was born.

McGivney's birth coincided neatly with the end of the pioneering era in American Catholicism, when regular services could be found only in cities as big as Boston, Hartford, New York, or Baltimore. At the same time, his youth fell almost exactly in line with the beginning of the Church's era of explosive growth in the United States.

Growth meant excitement and change, along with hard work, perhaps too much of it. For the following forty years, when large populations were moving to America from Catholic countries in Europe, as well as from Canada and Mexico, there would never be quite enough priests on hand to meet the many responsibilities placed upon them. Sacred duties were only the beginning. New immigrants typically looked to the parish priest for advice on a range of topics well beyond spiritual matters. Among them were the ever perplexing practicalities of the American way of life. Those who joined the priesthood in America during those demanding years were the type of men who would, if they were doctors, rush into the midst of an epidemic, or if they were soldiers, volunteer for the front line. Father O'Neile was one of them, as he gathered together the Catholic community in Waterbury. And that community constituted Michael McGivney's whole universe. He wouldn't know anything beyond it until he was well into his teens.

Michael grew up in the security of a strong family, both his own and that of the extended family of McGivneys and Lynches all around Waterbury. In all, Patrick and Mary McGivney would have twelve children,[7] seven of whom would survive infancy and grow up with Michael.

For Patrick McGivney, life in the cottage was ideal. Father Joseph Daley, who was acquainted with the family in later years, depicted Patrick by writing that he was "a sturdy iron-molder by trade and in his leisure something of an agriculturist."[8] Along the bank of the Naugatuck River, there was always room for more gardens, and children.

Mary McGivney, for her part, was intensely interested in the education of her family. That presented something of a challenge in Waterbury in the mid-1850s. The city had only one public school and none in proximity to the Irish community—either literally or figuratively. For Catholics and other non-Protestants, public schools in the mid-nineteenth century presented an uncomfortable alliance of church and state. Textbooks typically promoted Protestant teachings and often went so far as to disparage other beliefs. It wasn't an attractive prospect for families such as the McGivneys, but in Waterbury, as in hundreds of other American municipalities, there wasn't any choice in the matter.

Admission to public school in Waterbury normally occurred when a child was about six. Mary McGivney wasn't sure what would happen when her oldest, Michael, reached that age in 1858, but in the meantime, she saw no reason for him or his siblings to wait. She began teaching them as soon as they were able to open a book, or pick up a piece of chalk. Nonetheless, the McGivneys were going to need a school. Hundreds of other immigrant families in Waterbury already did need one.

In 1853, when Michael McGivney was still a baby, sleeping while his parents sat in the pews during Mass at St. Peter's, Bishop O'Reilly traveled to Ireland in search of more priests, ones willing to serve in southern New England. At the time, O'Reilly's Hartford Diocese included all of Connecticut, Rhode Island, and a small part of southeastern Massachusetts. It did not, however, have a seminary. Only a few seminaries in the United States were operating then, and they were as yet producing a mere handful of new priests each year. In the earlier, pioneering era, America's Catholic priests had typically been imported from France, but by the 1850s, the vast majority were from Ireland.

In practical terms, the Irish clergymen were welcomed because they spoke English and so could connect to the widest possible community. Moreover, they brought impressive credentials. The entrance exam for Ireland's predominant seminary, St. Patrick's College at Maynooth, was rigorous. For those who were admitted, the level of study was on a par with

that of Trinity University in Dublin, which was itself on a par
with either Oxford or Cambridge. Irish priests were well prepared, but more to the point, they were readily available. Between 1845 and 1854, approximately 1 million Irish people
died of starvation and 1.6 million others emigrated, most to
the United States. In losing nearly one-third of its population,
the isle was left with something of a surplus of trained priests.

The Irish domination of the U.S. Catholic Church grew
into a self-perpetuating proposition during the nineteenth
century, as Irish priests were naturally inclined to recruit more
Irish priests. From 1850 to 1870, the priesthood in America
barely expanded at all except through the arrival of ships from
Ireland.

The constant search for new priests motivated Bishop
O'Reilly's 1853 trip to Ireland, where he duly paid a call at
Maynooth. It was there that he met Thomas Hendricken, a
young dynamo of unswerving faith. Hendricken would become a figure of lasting influence in Michael McGivney's life
and in his perception of the Church as an instrument of Jesus
Christ.

A native of Kilkenny, in the east of Ireland, Thomas Hendricken was half-German. He was twenty-six when he finished his studies at Maynooth, and during the lull just after his
graduation, but before his ordination, he wasn't quite sure
what to do. He wanted a challenge, a chance to create something great and permanent. Many of the people escaping the
deteriorating conditions in Ireland felt the same way. When
Bishop O'Reilly arrived at Maynooth, Hendricken was
weighing the idea of joining a mission in the Far East.
O'Reilly, for his part, approached his recruiting mission with

unusually high standards. Despite the demand for parish priests in the United States, he was not looking for just any sort of person. Good health was a singularly important requisite. American priests could count on the constant stress of overwork, as well as the danger of frequent visitations in quarters racked with disease. Far from being remote or effete figures, parish priests were expected to be towers of strength, available to parishioners every day of the week.

Father Hendricken was at first glance an intelligent-looking man: bespectacled and smooth-faced, with a prominent, arching nose. But anyone could see that he was hardly robust. In fact, he suffered from occasional bouts of asthma. They didn't stop him, however, and neither did anything else. In Hendricken, Bishop O'Reilly spotted a man not only equal to the challenges ahead, but one who seemed in some sense to require them. He soon convinced Hendricken that the opportunity to serve God was just as great in Connecticut as in any outpost in China. Before Hendricken even set sail for America, he was ordained for the diocese of Hartford by Bishop O'Reilly.

Father Hendricken's journey to America was to become the stuff of legend in New England. While the young priest was traveling on an upper deck in the cabin class of the ship, a contagious disease swept through steerage, leaving passengers there at the point of death. Father Hendricken felt it his duty to see them, despite the captain's explicit orders that no one pass between the two classes.

On transatlantic ships, families of ten or twelve sometimes lived in steerage quarters so tight that "stand sleeping" was the norm. Disease swept easily through such abysmal compartments.

That was the situation into which Father Hendricken plunged, against captain's orders, on his crossing in 1853.

Perhaps young Father Hendricken was overly anxious to save souls, being newly ordained, but save them he certainly did as he moved through the squalid quarters. His reward for his selflessness, however, was something of a surprise. No sooner did he come up from the steerage compartment than he was arrested and locked in his cabin.

The rumor went around the ship that the infuriated captain intended to put the priest into a sack and throw him overboard. Many people onboard regarded the captain's attitude as anti-Catholic—although the seaman was actually far ahead of the medical science of his time, in quarantining the priest after his exposure in steerage to germs (a word not yet known in 1853). In any case, Father Hendricken suffered the remainder of the long voyage believing that at any moment he would be put in a sack and drowned. That sort of thing wears on even the most righteous. When the ship finally landed in New York, though, the young priest was still aboard. In later years, he came to regard the captain's change of heart as a providential occurrence.[9]

In 1855, the year Michael McGivney turned three, Father Hendricken was assigned to take over St. Peter's Church in Waterbury. He would spend the next seventeen years there. Hendricken would be the first parish priest that McGivney ever really knew and, indeed, the only person that McGivney looked to as pastor until the day he left Waterbury.

From the first, Hendricken realized that the bishop had

been right back at Maynooth: for Catholics, the situation in America was as dire as it was anywhere in the world. As Father Hendricken settled into his new surroundings in Waterbury, he could readily see how great the need was—especially when he couldn't even see all of his parishioners. At Mass on Sundays, people not only filled the pews but overflowed onto the steps outside and filled part of the road. Cold as it was sometimes, they prayed with Father Hendricken, even if it meant they had to kneel in the mud.[10] Out of sheer sympathy, he no doubt prayed a little bit more quickly in winter than in spring or summer.

Under Father Hendricken's guidance, the parish quickly completed plans for a larger church. In the summer of 1857, the cornerstone was laid amid great ceremony. While Bishop O'Reilly watched, two hundred children from the Sunday school paraded past the new site. Michael McGivney, just a month shy of his fifth birthday, was almost certainly among them. The dedication of the new church, to be called Immaculate Conception, would affect young Michael as much as anyone else present, not so much because it opened, but because in its wake, St. Peter's closed.

Father Hendricken wasn't through with the old St. Peter's. He immediately established a grade school in the basement, relying on erudite members of his parish to do the teaching. Occasionally, the most sophisticated of them all, Father Hendricken himself, would take over a class. While religion was introduced at appropriate times during the day, Father Hendricken leaned away from making the school parochial in the strict sense. It even became known as the East

Main Street School, rather than St. Peter's. In 1860, the Waterbury Board of Education was so impressed with the little institution that it took over the whole operation, making the schooling free for the predominantly Catholic population in the vicinity. It was an admirably tolerant gesture for the time. An open school was just what Father Hendricken had always had in mind. Until Immaculate Conception could truly run a school system of its own, he wanted to ensure that all of his children had the best possible chance at an education. Before the cunning Father Hendricken was through, he even had the city paying rent to the parish for the use of the building.

Father Hendricken made a vivid impression in Waterbury, as the leader of the Catholic community there. "Only those who knew [Hendricken] intimately could appreciate the nobility of his character," a colleague once wrote. "No man was more approachable. He received rich and poor alike with an easy grace that left no room for the self-assertion of the one or a tinge of servility in the other.

"He would never say No when it was possible to say Yes," Hendricken's friend continued, "but when circumstances demanded prompt decision, no one could display more firmness of character."[11] For McGivney and others in the parish, Father Hendricken was a figure of stability, intellect, and self-respect, qualities not always easy to find in the beleaguered Irish Catholic community.

In 1859, when Michael McGivney was six, he duly took the entrance examination for the East Main Street School and astonished the teachers by scoring well enough to skip the first two grades. Placed in the third grade, he was quite a joy

to have in the classroom, according to a 1901 article written
with the cooperation of people who knew him in his school
days: "The principal, Thomas Meagher, was charmed with
the boy's manner and from the date of his entrance into the
class room until he had gone through the different grades he
was noted for excellent deportment and proficiency in his
studies."[12]

Studying in the basement of St. Peter's by day and attending Mass and other services at Immaculate Conception
all through the week, Michael McGivney practically grew
up in the Church. Next to his parents, the most important
adult in his life was his parish priest. And perhaps the parish
priest was even more influential in young McGivney's case.
When he was about twelve, the boy expressed his earnest
wish to join the priesthood. His father was adamantly
against the idea.

Patrick McGivney was devout in his Catholicism, but he
remained unconvinced that the priesthood was right for his
oldest son. Perhaps he felt that Michael was just too young to
make any far-reaching decisions about his future. In any
case, as Reverend Daley related, Patrick "would not lend
himself to encouraging in his son any such preference and,
when in due time solicited, absolutely refused to grant pater-
nal sanction."[13]

In the Waterbury schools, students were typically sixteen
years old when they graduated. Michael McGivney, however,
had been accelerated so many times that he was only thirteen
when he left East Main Street School. With his family growing ever larger with the passing years, money was tight at

home. Michael did his part to help and placated his father at the same time by taking a factory job, helping to make spoons at a Waterbury concern called Holmes, Booth and Haydens. For the time being, he kept his feeling about his place in the priesthood to himself.

3

THE PRIESTHOOD

What would make a kid of twelve or thirteen so certain that he wanted to be a priest?

Coming of age during the Civil War, Michael McGivney might easily have wanted to be a soldier instead. Or he could have harbored plans to go out west. People from every community east of the Mississippi did just that, and enough of them brought back fortunes that the temptation to try the frontier was ever present in a factory town like Waterbury.

Across southern New England, every boy was susceptible to the lure of the sea, if only as a chance to travel for a while. The bustle of commerce in Boston to the north and New York City to the south beckoned in the same way. A fellow as bright as McGivney could even have prepared to become a college man: a diplomat, doctor, or lawyer. Other first-generation Americans managed it. McGivney could have, too.

But as he entered his teens, McGivney wasn't drawn to seek a fortune or even to see the world. He wanted to continue the course he was no doubt already on: to become during his life just as an apostle of Jesus. According to the gospel of John, anyone who truly loves Jesus is given His friendship, but a priest is asked to give even more, and likewise, he receives even more.

James Cardinal Gibbons, the archbishop of Baltimore from 1877 until his death in 1921, was only eighteen years older than McGivney and his experience foreshadowed that of McGivney in some respects.[1] Their middle-class, Irish-American backgrounds were similar and Gibbons also decided to join the priesthood while he was in his teens. Unlike Michael McGivney, however, he did flirt with another course in life and, in fact, had another attractive opportunity practically pressed on him.

Gibbons had been born in Baltimore of Irish parents, but the whole family moved back to Ireland when his father's health failed. Upon his father's death, his mother decided to return to America, putting the family on a ship bound for Baltimore. It never arrived, sinking somewhere off the Bahamas. The Gibbons family, among the lucky few to be rescued, ended up in New Orleans. Quick to learn, with a sunny personality and an abundance of energy, James Gibbons soon worked his way up in the wholesale-food business. At nineteen, he had the backing of a wealthy mentor and the promise of a very prosperous future. At that juncture, though, and despite all sorts of enticements from his boss, Gibbons decided to resign in order to study for the priesthood.

Gibbons never forgot the sense of privilege with which he approached a future in the Church. The priest, he wrote, "not only represents Christ, but *personates* Him and becomes identical with Him in his ministerial functions, as far as two personalities can be considered identical.

"The priest," Gibbons marveled, "not only acts with Christ, by the authority of Christ, in the name of Christ, but his official acts are Christ's acts. His words are the echo of Christ's voice."[2]

As even young McGivney could plainly see, however, a priest also shared Christ's sacrifices and a measure of his pain. This aspect of the special communion with Christ took various forms—but a priest could take satisfaction in perceiving that with each act of devotion or sacrifice, especially the most taxing, he lifted a small weight of the Savior's load. Each time he celebrated Mass, he would feel it. And then on through the day: in the round-the-clock obligation to call upon the sick and troubled, he would shoulder burdens that defeated all others, and try not to break under the strain.

In comparing martyrs and priests, St. John Chrysostom (c. 347–407) observed that martyrs die only once for Jesus Christ, while the pastor of souls must die daily for his flock.[3] Whenever that was the case, the priest's life overlapped with that of his Savior, to whom was given by all accounts the hardest life of all on earth.

As young Michael McGivney was aware, another aspect of the priest's life was the vow of celibacy. It has been regarded as the most conspicuous aspect of the priest's sacrifice, especially in recent times. In the mid-nineteenth century, however, the emphasis was not placed so much on the fact that the priest could not marry and the narrow construct that follows—that he couldn't have a sexual life with a woman. The import of the vow, as it was discussed then, was placed instead along its broader context: the challenge for the priest of cultivating his emotions, such that he would remain pure of passions, tempers, temptations, and vices of any kind. "He makes a vow, not of conjugal but of virginal chastity," noted Cardinal Gibbons. "He must be pure not only in body, but in mind, heart, and affection also."[4]

If there were people in the general population who considered such purity in a man as "unnatural," those within the Church might be surprisingly willing to agree. The priestly life was not natural—except for those called to it. For them, it was indeed super-natural. By no means just another job, the priesthood was instead a state of being, somewhere between earth and heaven. And the harder a priest worked at the many aspects of service, of sacrifice, and an abiding emulation of Jesus Christ, the more familiar he would become with heaven, even in his years on earth. That was a heady prospect for a devout young Catholic like McGivney.

In his first letter to the Corinthians, St. Paul called priests the "stewards of the mysteries of God." Other Catholic believers may have rejoiced in the bond between God and man, but priests actually occupied that bond. To some of them, serving for decades, their place of work was not unlike the ladder Jacob described in his dream, the one that angels used in order to take messages back and forth between humans and the Lord. More typically, though, the bond was perceived less literally.

Jacques Millet, another priest who came of age in the mid-nineteenth century, was unable to describe the role of the priest in exact terms—which is precisely what inspired him most. "At the altar in Holy Mass," Millet wrote, "it is Jesus Christ who offers gifts, changes the bread and wine into His own Body and Blood, and immolates the victim. As Jesus Christ and the Church, according to St. Augustine, are not two Christs, but one Christ, so the Eternal Priest and all priests born in time are not a multitude of priests, but one Priest. The man disappears in this August mystery."

"His personality," Millet continued, "is converted into that of the Man-God, who gives him the power to say at the moment of consecration: *This is My Body.*"[5]

In addition to having sole responsibility for offering the sacrifice of the Mass, priests were granted the ability to absolve sin. No one who was not an extension of the Lord could do that, and except under extraordinary circumstances, no one except a priest was allowed to act for Him.

To a pure-hearted Catholic, abilities like that made a fellow more powerful than anyone, including the president—any president. Even if some of the other kids in Waterbury didn't quite see it that way, it was true in the eyes of Michael McGivney. And while a priest was not entitled to entertain the passion of worldly ambition, it could not be lost on a young man considering the priesthood that he would, if ordained, be a force in a community, a force that might even outlast his own life on earth.

Father Millet made another observation that presaged Michael McGivney's life: "It is Jesus Christ who lives and acts in the priest. That is why he has power to reform and to make perfect, not only individuals, but entire nations, for his is pre-eminently a civilizing influence. . . . All institutions religious in character, all moral and philanthropic associations, not touched by the hand of the priest and vivified by his breath, languish, wither and die."[6]

The opportunity to join in an internal way with the Holy Family and extend Its powers on earth may have been the primary appeal of the priesthood for a boy with the depth of belief of Michael McGivney. But then there was that other aspect of living as truly as possible as a brother of Christ: moral leadership within a community of very human, human beings, both believers and skeptics—and most important, perhaps, those who were wavering between the two. In the 1880s, Old Wolf, a Cheyenne chief from Montana, told this story:

In the land of the Cheyennes, there is a mountain higher than all the mountains around him. All the Cheyennes know that mountain; even our forefathers knew him. When children, we ran around wheresoever we wanted. We were never afraid to lose our way so long as we could see that mountain, which would show us home again. When grown up, we followed the buffalo and the elk; we cared not where we pursued the running deer, so long as the mountain was in sight; for we knew he was ever a safe guide, and never failed in his duty. When men, we fought the Sioux, the Crows, the white men. We went after the enemy, though the way ran high up, and low down. Our hearts trembled not on account of the road; for as long as we could see the mountain, we felt sure of finding our home again. When far away, our hearts leaped for joy on seeing him, because he told us that our home came nearer.

During the winter, the snow covered all the earth with a mantle of white; we could no longer distinguish him from other mountains except by his height, which told us he was *the* mountain. Sometimes dark clouds gathered above. They hid his head from our view, and out of them flew fiery darts, boring holes in his sides. The thunder shook him from head to foot; but the storm passed away and the mountain stood forever.

This mountain is the Black-robe.* His heart is firm as a rock. He changes not. He speaks to us the words of truth. We are always sure of our path, when we look to him for guidance. He is the mountain that leads us up to God.

It was in order to stand as firm as Old Wolf's mountain that the parish priest made his vows and his sacrifices. Without any turbulence in his own heart, he might just be as dependable and as strong.

That was the ideal and in nineteenth-century America, the ideal of the priestly life was as strong as ever it has been. The high regard for the "priest as [a] sacral figure set apart"[7] did not arise from mere naïveté on the part of the flock, however. The many high-powered men who were drawn to the

---

*A Native American expression for a Roman Catholic priest.

priesthood believed with a kind of determination in the ideal, protecting it with their deeds, and not just words. A historian writing in 1912 of the development of America's clerics during the previous half century made the point that "priestly character was moulded by daily intercourse with the self-sacrificing pioneer bishops and priests."[8]

In Catholic communities, especially the immigrant ones, the priest was regarded as the ultimate authority figure. As the oldest child in a large family, Michael McGivney was well equipped to fill that role. He was a natural leader, not in the outgoing, ebullient manner of James Gibbons, but in his own quietly supportive style. He could hope to become a "Father" in the world of his fellow Catholics. But whether he would make the grade, succeeding through to ordination, was far from a settled issue. The educational requirements for the priesthood were extremely demanding in the mid-nineteenth century. A seminary course, heavy on courses in classics and philosophy, took six years. In terms of the length of study and its difficulty, the Catholic standard for ordained priests was on a par with the requirements for new physicians.

Even so, many older priests wanted the seminaries to add a year of study and make the overall course even harder.[9] As urgent as the demand for new priests may have been, the prevailing philosophy was that it would be better to lose a few barely qualified candidates than to accept any unqualified ones.

The Roman Catholic Church was very much on the defensive in the United States in the decades following the 1840s, when anti-Catholic fervor stopped just short of igniting an outright religious war. With increased immigration, a "nativist" movement coalesced around prejudice against Catholics, in particular, often on the supposition that the pope commanded more loyalty from them than the U.S. president. Rising hatreds resulted in anti-Catholic riots, notably in Philadelphia in 1844, when the violence lasted three days.[10] Parish priests, with their air of mystery, were particularly despised by the bigoted members of the "Know-Nothing" Party and their many unaffiliated sympathizers. The Know-Nothing Party was actually a collection of secret societies that rose to the fore in the Northeast in the 1850s to promote nativism and to fight immigration, particularly that of Roman Catholics. When leaders of other political parties tried to investigate such societies, in order to harness the votes of the members, they invariably received the same answer: individuals claimed to "know nothing." The Know-Nothings grew in influence, though, inciting sporadic attacks on Catholics throughout the country.[11] Bishop O'Reilly of the Hartford Diocese was commonly jeered as "Paddy the Priest" by the children of Know-Nothing parents.[12]

In 1855, the anti-Catholic movement came out into the open and became institutionalized with the launch of the American Party. Members nominated former president Millard Fillmore to head their ticket in 1856. Immediately powerful, the party reached out to the South, where nativism flourished. The South would seem to have been fertile territory, yet it proved to be the undoing of the American Party. Southern Know-Nothings insisted that protection of slavery be a part of the official platform; Northerners, even bigoted ones, couldn't accept that plank and the party fell apart. The hatreds that it planted, however, did not die quite so quickly.

Bishops and other Roman Catholic leaders were keenly aware that priests were under close scrutiny in the uncomfortable peace that followed the Know-Nothing years. The Church could ill afford any kind of bellicose, ignorant, or, worse yet, scandalous behavior that might fuel the prejudices still lying under the surface in America. As with any group fighting for its place in a new land, the Catholics of the last half of the nineteenth century had to be above reproach—and the priests, in particular, had to be perfect.

They weren't perfect, of course. But through the years they did not sully the ideal. The bishops who selected students for seminary and then graduates for ordination showed scant tolerance for any slight character flaws they might detect. In addition to final exams in school, the man who became a priest had to pass a very long and careful test of just exactly who he was and what he wanted to do with the gift of the priesthood.

As a result, the parish priest loomed large in the eyes of his parishioners. No sooner did he adopt his uniform cassock (the Roman collar would not be instituted until 1884) than he would be counted on as a man of erudition, trusted even by the most cynical.[13] For a teenager considering the priesthood, that was certainly an intriguing prospect. A lawyer had to build a practice before handling a really important case. A budding professor started out by correcting papers and washing lab equipment. But a priest commenced his first day with all the glory he would ever have, and all he could ever want. More, the priesthood offered the opportunity to attain a spiritual state as close to God as a Catholic could hope to have while still on earth.

Such righteous possibilities might naturally make a sober, smart, and devout young man like Michael McGivney want to be a priest. But there was more to it than wanting. The calling had to come from God. That characteristic, so easy to fake at least for a while, was the one that the bishops were at pains to discern before letting a man enter the priesthood. "Vocation to the priesthood is a providential act," Cardinal Gibbons wrote insistently, "by which God selects some persons in preference to others for the work of the ministry, and confers on them particular graces for its faithful execution."[14] Gibbons recalled one young man who stated frankly that he wanted to be a priest for the simple reason that he didn't like work. That fellow didn't pass muster, but then, if he didn't like work, he was in the wrong place anyway.

Bishops were also on the lookout to purge candidates who were seeking orders only in deference to the wishes of one or both parents.[15] The calling had to come from the Lord, not from the other end of the dining table. Michael McGivney didn't fall into that category by any means. He wanted to become a priest despite parental pressure, not because of it.

At the age of sixteen, Michael was certain of how he felt. He had had three years to mull it over as he helped turn out spoons at Holmes, Booth and Haydens. It was not that he wanted to be a priest. It was that he had to be one. The calling was there.

Patrick McGivney could see by then that the idea was no passing fancy. He gave his son permission to turn to a new life, the one once described as "in the world, but not of the world."

In September 1868, Michael McGivney took leave of

Waterbury and separated from his family for the first time. As he must have been reminded a hundred times in the weeks leading up to his departure, he could always return home if he wanted. But the whole idea, and his reason for leaving, was to be nurtured into a new family. In the company of Father Hendricken, Michael McGivney left on a train bound for Canada, where he was to be enrolled as a student at the Seminary of St.-Hyacinthe.

4

A START IN SEMINARY

In all, Father Hendricken escorted eleven boys from the Hartford Diocese on the train to Canada, where they were to start their studies.[1] None of them could be blamed if they were still a little surprised to find themselves heading for the Seminary of St.-Hyacinthe. Typically, boys from Connecticut who wanted to study for the priesthood gravitated to Maryland, the location of St. Charles College.

St. Charles was a "minor" seminary, a six-year prep school specifically designed in its coursework as well as its atmosphere to feed students into a "major" or vocational seminary. In modern terms, it was equivalent to high school and two years of college.[2] Graduates could go on to a nonreligious profession if they chose, but in the case of most St. Charles students, the next stop was St. Mary's Seminary in Baltimore, the oldest Catholic seminary in the United States, founded in 1791, when George Washington was president.

St. Mary's and its little brother, St. Charles, held a privileged place, being intertwined with the Baltimore Archdiocese, the official seat of American Catholicism. Although American bishops had long resisted a movement to create a national seminary, setting the goal instead that each diocese produce its own priests in its own schools, for many people, St. Mary's assumed the position of the nation's leading seminary. It had impeccable standards of learning, but more than that, it was in step with the evolution of American Catholicism. And that was precisely why Michael McGivney was headed in the opposite direction, toward Canada, with the band of other Connecticut boys.

Church leaders might convene provincial councils every decade or so to guide the Church in America. Ecclesiastical scholars could debate the influences over the Church as it grew and the instant traditions imprinted upon it by the dominant Irish clergy. But they weren't the real experts on the emerging American personality of the Catholic Church, not in the experience of the Reverend Francis McFarland, Bishop O'Reilly's successor as the head of the Hartford Diocese. To him, the most sensitive authority on American-styled Catholicism seemed to be just about any French-Canadian parishioner, newly arrived in southern New England. The local churches just didn't feel right to French-Canadians, and they let their priests know it.

Bishop McFarland was acutely aware that thousands of such French-Canadians were pouring into his diocese, drawn by New England's manufacturing boom. Always an activist, he was determined to greet them with priests well versed in their language and their ways.[3]

Since the Hartford Diocese had no seminary of its own, Bishop McFarland was obligated to steer budding theologians elsewhere. In 1868, facing the choice of ordering up a future class of either standard American priests from a place like St. Charles College or worldly Quebecois ones from an equivalent minor seminary in Canada, he knew full well what the situation required—and would demand as the years went by. His aim was to send willing young men to St.-Hyacinthe in the province of Quebec.

As Bishop McFarland spread the word of his inclination to send diocesan youth to study in Canada, Father Hendricken in Waterbury responded in his usual way: he made it happen. In his own parish, he had cultivated eleven young men with a serious interest in the priesthood. (If every parish had offered the same number, the Catholic Church would have had a surplus of clerics, rather than a shortage.) Father Hendricken's charisma and his example no doubt contributed to the bumper crop, but on a practical level, he may well have assisted some of the poorer boys with expenses or even tuition.

The somber city of St. Hyacinthe lies thirty-five miles southeast of Montreal, across the St. Lawrence River. In the late nineteenth century, the population of ten thousand was 90 percent Catholic, with more than a thousand men and women living in various religious communities, including several different convents and a monastery.[4] The seminary offered both minor and major studies, although many students switched schools after finishing their minor-seminary work and took their major course at Montreal's well-respected Sainte-Marie College.

Only forty miles from the Vermont border and a one-day train ride from Connecticut, St.-Hyacinthe suited Bishop McFarland's ulterior motive perfectly. Sending Michael McGivney and the other boys there was an excellent plan, except for one thing—as pleased as McFarland was to think that his Yankees would be immersed in French-Canadian culture, the administrators at St.-Hyacinthe were just as delighted with an entirely different scheme of their own.

McGivney and his classmates from the Hartford Diocese found themselves in a special section at St.-Hyacinthe, with classes taught predominantly in English by a faculty of fifteen priests from Ireland. The school encouraged the activities of its St. Patrick Association and made an overt holiday of March 17. For the American students, St.-Hyacinthe smacked as much of Tipperary as of Quebec.

Bishop McFarland may have had his goal—to develop priests sensitive to French-Canadian needs—but St.-Hyacinthe had an agenda, too. "Let us say," a seminarian reflected, "that the directors knew how to initiate a *modus vivendi,* a truly acceptable climate for the foreign students."[5] The school wanted graduates who became parish priests one day to send potential seminarians back to the friendly old alma mater.

Michael McGivney, for one, seemed to find the surroundings at St.-Hyacinthe entirely comfortable. He joined various religious societies at the school—in piety, of course, but also because he was aware that anyone who didn't belong to one sodality or another was jeered at by the other students as a "Franc-maçon" (a Freemason).[6] At a time when the Freemasons were virulently anti-Catholic, it was a stinging insult, tempered only by its absurdity in the halls of a Roman Catholic seminary. With or without peer pressure, McGivney was on the rolls of the Sodality of the Holy Angels in his first year, and in his second he was in the Sodality of the Blessed Virgin.

McGivney must have found enjoyment in the companionship of his fellow students from Waterbury, but he was very shy as a teenager. Although he made friends easily throughout his life, he was never known to be extroverted. That was especially true at St.-Hyacinthe, where he approached his studies with a flinty determination that didn't leave time for much else.

The greatest problem facing McGivney, as with many of the new boys from America, was ascertaining just what exactly he knew. Public schools in America did not then have standardized curricula, so the teachers at St.-Hyacinthe had to situate the new students in courses that picked up wherever their former education left off. Waterbury's public school was almost certainly light on the classical languages. McGivney may or may not have been exposed to Latin—but he would have to be fluent in it before he could attend a major seminary. He would also need to understand ancient Greek. The other courses typically required for admission into a major seminary were English, another modern language, Christian doctrine, rhetoric, elocution, history, geography, math, science, bookkeeping, and Gregorian chant.[7]

In July 1870, McGivney was completing his second year

at St.-Hyacinthe. According to the list of school honors printed just as he left for his summer vacation in Waterbury, he was the recipient of the Prize of Excellence, in recognition of his "studiousness" and "application." Each course also had individual awards. McGivney took a first prize in English themes (writing) and second prizes in both grammar and the interpretation of English authors.

McGivney's record was stellar—but when looked at closely, his best subjects were those centered on his native language. While he was obviously putting in an effort, he may have been lagging in Latin and Greek. Of course, one could look at the scant remains of his record at St.-Hyacinthe and note as easily that he didn't stand out in math or Gregorian chanting, either, for that matter. Those subjects, however, were not quite so essential to success at a major seminary and, perchance, to the work of a priest in the years after that.

That summer, Michael McGivney decided not to return to St.-Hyacinthe. After a yearlong break, he resumed his studies at the Seminary of Our Lady of Angels in Niagara Falls, New York, arriving in September 1871.[8] An advertisement like the following, written by the president of the school, Reverend Robert Rice, may have helped to snag the nineteen-year-old:

> This institution, situated . . . four miles from the Falls of Niagara, overlooks the famous Niagara River, and commands an extensive view of its sublime and varied scenery. With the grandeur and beauty of location, it also enjoys the great advantage of salubrity of climate. The Seminary possesses a large farm, a considerable

portion of which is allotted to the Students for recreation grounds.[9]

Robert Emmett Rice, the head of the school, was born on a plantation in Missouri and educated for the priesthood in France. He was only twenty-six when he took charge of the Seminary of Our Lady of Angels in 1863.[10] It was then operating in the property's original farmhouse. Many seminaries in the United States were as humble then, catering to five or ten students at a time. Before the decade was out, however, Father Rice had built a thriving school, complete with respectably huge campus buildings. His charisma, the institution's most valuable asset, was born of the trust that he placed in nearly everyone he met. His conviction that no one would abuse that trust allowed him to be just a bit indulgent, and in that respect he became a model for students like Michael McGivney. As one seminarian wrote of the celebrated president, "Encouraging every project that might tend to the amusement or improvement of the students, Father Rice sanctioned the formation of literary and dramatic associations, of religious societies and athletic clubs. . . . As time advanced the number of students increased."[11]

McGivney may have craved the bracing fresh air of Our Lady of Angels. But he certainly needed to bolster his knowledge of the classics and fill in other philosophy courses before he could be considered ready for admission to a major theological seminary. In fact, Our Lady of Angels was itself a full-scale seminary in that sense, but Michael McGivney does not seem to have regarded it as such. He was still in the preparatory stage of his education for the priesthood.

Meanwhile, Father Hendricken was continuing his knack for guiding young men into the priesthood. In addition to McGivney, three other men from Waterbury started in 1871 at Our Lady of Angels (which was also then known as Niagara College and later officially renamed Niagara University). They joined the many Waterbury residents already on the school roster. Statistically, there were five Waterburians for each student from any other municipality in Connecticut.[12]

One of those rare Connecticut boys who didn't spring from Waterbury was James P. Splain of New Haven. Like Mc-Givney, he had begun his studies in Quebec. Whether or not the two met there, they became fast friends in Niagara. Splain was also at the school to focus on classical studies, even though he had already left behind thoughts of the priesthood in favor of a career in medicine. Known for his spirit of fun, he was described as "genial, companionable and sociable, with a ready wit and sense of humor."[13] McGivney was likewise born with the ability to make people laugh and lift their spirits, but as a young adult, he adopted instead a scholarly remove. Perhaps it seemed more dignified and "priestly." The lively days with James Splain helped to bring out—or bring back—McGivney's ready humor.

Another of McGivney's close friends at the seminary was Edward Antill, possibly the brightest student at the school. Antill was just as irrepressible outside of the classroom as inside, joining a wide array of Niagara's extracurricular clubs. From the Literary Association to the Choral Union, he was an all-around booster on campus.[14]

Antill's only rival in that realm was John J. Splain, James's younger brother, who would never become an ordained priest—but who certainly had a good time at the seminary. Among other things, John was president of the Billiard Association and a dedicated baseball fanatic. But then, so was Edward Antill. Practically everyone at the Seminary of Our Lady of Angels was a little bit distracted by baseball. The sport was in the ascendancy throughout the country in the 1870s, with professional teams forming in many northeastern cities. At Niagara, all of the baseball games were intramural, between teams formed by particular groups of students. Father Charles V. Eckles, a nationally known scholar in his day, was faculty advisor to one of the teams. And when the reigning champions of the campus, the Mont Eagles, refused a challenge from the upstart Niagaras with a terse and rather condescending memo, the Niagaras went straight to the president of the seminary, Father Rice. They found him in his private quarters and asked him to intercede, which he did, forcing the Mont Eagles to take the field (where they suffered a drubbing).[15] Every year on June 2, Father Rice's birthday was celebrated with a day off for the students featuring, at the president's request, ball games, among other activities.

Sports of all kinds were intrinsic to Our Lady of Angels, which made it fairly unique for a seminary. "We have had fellows whose strength of body reminded one of draught horses," recalled a priest on the faculty, referring to McGivney's era, "and fellows whose physical weakness caused them to cough between commas while reciting an *Ave Maria*. Each of these classes had to have its suitable recreation, with ample provision for that middle class whose members may be strong enough, but who are not hazardous enough, to indulge in brisk encounter."[16]

In terms of athletic ability, McGivney was deceptive. He stood about five foot ten—which was quite tall for his day. As a point of comparison, the champion Niagaras team of 1871 featured only one player who was taller than that, at five foot eleven. (The average was five foot eight.)[17] McGivney, however, didn't have much muscle and didn't necessarily look the part of a draft horse. Someone nonetheless found out that he was a naturally talented ballplayer.

It might have been his friend on the faculty, Reverend Eckles.[18] It might have been Edward Antill, who was a good pitcher himself. Most likely, it was his pal John J. Splain, who was organizing a new team in early 1872, the Charter Oaks. In those days, a ball club only had nine players, with no substitutes.

John was the president and the pitcher. Richard O'Grady, another member of the Waterbury contingent, played second base. McGivney was in left field. While that isn't necessarily a "skill" position in today's fenced-in baseball fields, it indicated in the world of 1872 baseball that he could run fast and throw the ball a long way. He was probably one of the three fastest runners on the team, in fact. In the high-scoring games of the early 1870s, playing on unenclosed fields, the outfielders were often forced to chase the ball a long, long way. And Our Lady of Angels had that "large farm" on which to play. The ball could roll for miles, or so it might seem to the left fielder.

The Charter Oaks scheduled their first game for May 20, 1872, answering a challenge from the Mohawks. According to the box score printed in the school paper, the *Index Niagarensis,* John Splain pitched a good game, holding the Mohawks in check the whole way. He also scored twice. McGivney did even better, crossing home plate three times. The Charter Oaks ultimately won, 23–6.[19]

The Charter Oaks remained undefeated, in as much as *Index* did not record that they ever played another game. That doesn't mean that McGivney was through with the sport, however. He may well have played in one of the pickup games that sprang up on Father Rice's birthday in June. That afternoon, so the paper reported, "the students patronized base-ball, the mazes of the scup, mumble-the-peg, or other exhilarating exercises."[20] Regrettably, the *Index* did not print box scores for mumble-the-peg.

The emphasis on fresh air and outdoor sports that permeated the Seminary of Our Lady of Angels did not diminish its academic integrity. The classes were bracing, the quality of the professors high. There was a spirit about the place, however, that McGivney—that terribly serious, perhaps dangerously determined student of St.-Hyacinthe days—needed to take into his heart. "Niagara," wrote a professor wryly, "feeling that the taxed brain must be rested, that the physical man must be developed unless her students are to shrivel into intellectual coffins, has always provided them with amusements, more or less athletic, throughout the scholastic year."[21] It left McGivney with a simple lesson that every overly intense young priest must learn: it's all right to laugh.

McGivney didn't return to Our Lady of Angels in the autumn of 1872. He could have been swayed by the fact that, as an editorialist in the *Index* wrote, "the winter of '71–'72 was one of the longest and most severe experienced for some years."[22] But weather wasn't a real consideration. At the end of the 1871–72 term, McGivney received honorable mention in the commencement program for his work in five subjects, three of them in classical studies: Greek, Latin, translation (he was specifically cited for his work translating Livy), algebra, and composition.[23] With that, he was ready to focus his studies on preparation for the priesthood at a major seminary, and the one that he chose was Sainte-Marie in Montreal.

At home in Waterbury, Patrick McGivney was still working as a molder. He had long since left Merrit Nichols's factory, and was an employee of the larger Farrell Foundry and Machine Company. He had been in the industry for more than twenty years and had a reputation for being willing to share what he knew with younger workers. "Some of the best molders in Waterbury got their first knowledge of the business from him," recalled a city resident in 1900.[24] When Patrick left Merrit Nichols, he also gave up the appealing cottage he rented on the Naugatuck River, moving to a larger house at 5 Railroad Hill Street. Perhaps it was just as well; the family continued to grow. In fact, the youngest child, a boy named John, had been born while Michael was a student at St.-Hyacinthe.

In all, there were six McGivney children at home while Michael was away studying. Patrick earned steady wages at the foundry, dedicating his livelihood to his family. Even as he took good care of everyone at home, he also managed to spare more than three hundred dollars each year to pay for Michael's college expenses.[25]

When Michael came home in the summer of 1872, all was well with the McGivneys, but he was met with a dramatic change in his second home in Waterbury, the Immaculate Conception Church. Father Hendricken had moved away.

When Bishop McFarland's health began to fail in the early 1870s, the Holy See recognized that the Hartford Diocese had in fact grown too large for one man to administer. Rhode Island and the small portion of southeast Massachusetts that had been included in the Hartford Diocese were split off. In April 1872, Father Hendricken was consecrated as the first bishop of Providence.[26] While he was not entirely removed from Michael McGivney's life, he could no longer serve as a mentor.

By choosing to attend Sainte-Marie College in Montreal in the autumn of that same year, McGivney was finishing what he had started four years before, under Father Hendricken's tutelage, when he began his education in the province of Quebec. In another way, however, he was breaking yet new ground.

Some seminaries are operated by a certain diocese within the framework of the Church as a whole: St.-Hyacinthe, for example, was a diocesan institution. Other seminaries, however, fall within the province of a specific order (a religious community in which a particular aspect of Christian life is emphasized). Our Lady of Angels in Niagara Falls was operated by the Vincentians, an order that follows St. Vincent de Paul (1581–1660), in tending toward the consideration of the poorest and most troubled people in society. Montreal's Sainte-Marie College, on the other hand, was operated by the Jesuits, known for their intellectualism. Even though McGivney was a student there, he was not necessarily expected to join the Society of Jesus, the proper name of the Jesuit order.

Yet, according to an account written in 1900 by the Reverend Joseph Daley, who was later acquainted with Father Mc-Givney, the serious young Connecticut scholar was indeed planning to become a Jesuit.[27] Born with a fine mind and a great capacity for learning, he wanted to immerse himself in the most rigorous academic setting he could find. It was the inclination that Garry Wills, a former Jesuit seminarian, called "consecrating one's intellect to the service of God."[28] For Michael McGivney, the sternest test in the way of seminaries was Sainte-Marie College.

Through the fall of 1872 and into the following spring, McGivney studied in Montreal and was anticipating final exams in June. Perhaps it would be too much to say that he was *looking forward* to them, but they would demonstrate whether he was actually up to the level of Sainte-Marie's teaching—his most fervent concern. Or so he thought, in the isolated vanity of a student.

On June 6, 1873, Patrick McGivney died.

Michael left school without taking the exams. He packed his belongings, knowing that he would never return to Sainte-Marie, and went home to Railroad Hill Street in Waterbury. A family was reeling. He was reeling.

5

IN THE CITY OF NEW HAVEN

At the beginning of the summer of 1873, Michael Mc-Givney was faced with the prospect of finding a job in Waterbury to help support his mother and younger siblings. Money for tuition was no longer available. He couldn't return to Sainte-Marie.

After the initial disruption in the family finances, Michael's mother and oldest sisters carried on just the way Patrick Mc-Givney always had: by looking out for the others. The two oldest daughters, Mary and Rosanna, were employed, and between them, they could meet the household expenses.

At nineteen, Mary was engaged to a clerk named Michael Lawlor and would soon be married; as a couple, the two would continue to support the McGivney brood. Michael Lawlor was in a position to understand the sacrifices that families made to keep a seminarian on track: his two older brothers, Patrick and Martin, were already ordained priests. As new arrivals from Ireland in the 1850s, they had also been influenced and then mentored by Father Hendricken, that pied piper of Waterbury priests.[1] The Lawlor family had had its troubles, however. With the early deaths of both parents, the five boys had to support one another, and always did.

Even if the McGivney family could survive without Michael's financial support, it was not clear that he could survive without help from them—or someone. He still needed tuition in order to complete his theological studies. Word soon reached Bishop McFarland that McGivney, one of the diocese's most promising young men, required financial help.

With the bishop's intercession, the Hartford Diocese formally "adopted" McGivney as a student, granting him what amounted to a full scholarship, a concept otherwise little known at that time. Bishop McFarland, however, was not in favor of McGivney's returning to Sainte-Marie College in Montreal. The bishop had changed his mind about sending Irish-Americans from Connecticut to Quebec for their training. French-Canadian parishioners, as he discovered, were not fooled in the least; they only insisted even more vehemently with each passing year on having native French-speaking priests, either from Europe or Quebec. Moreover, Bishop McFarland was not quite so generous with diocesan funds that he would sponsor McGivney to become a Jesuit, one who might well disappear into another community. Since Bishop McFarland was on friendly terms with the president of St. Mary's Seminary in Baltimore, he made arrangements for McGivney to slide seamlessly into studies there, without losing credit for the year he had put in with the Jesuits in Montreal. On September 14, 1873, still in mourning for his father, Michael McGivney found himself settling once more into the sanctuary of his religious studies.

St. Mary's Seminary was operated by the Society of the Priests of St. Sulpice, an order founded in France in the seventeenth century. The Sulpicians have never been very well-known, except within the Catholic hierarchy, because their dominant mission has been to educate priests, specifically in the interest of helping bishops fill diocesan needs.

When McGivney arrived in Baltimore to begin his studies with the Sulpician faculty at St. Mary's, he had not entirely given up on his ambition to become a Jesuit scholar sometime in the future. He had, after all, regarded his previous schools as temporary stops. In the beginning, he didn't make a complete commitment to St. Mary's, either. Yet according to Father Joseph Daley, the Sulpicians offered just what McGivney needed:

> To them, he unfolded his mind anew, and they, finding in him the ideal vocation, diverted him entirely from the thought of joining the Jesuits. The arena of stirring toilers rather than that of placid thinkers was the sphere best adapted to qualities and energies such as were his, they argued; and so, while praising scholarship as a possession of great value, they taught him to regard it as merely a subsidiary quality in a priest—humanity, and not the humanities, should engage henceforth his most devoted study; sympathy for human woes was a property more intrinsic than knowledge; to store up

knowledge was good, they admitted: but to save souls was incomparably better.[2]

James Cardinal Gibbons, who had attended St. Mary's College a generation before McGivney, expressed the appeal of the teaching at his alma mater very simply. He wrote: "[I] shall never regret that I placed myself under the care of the Sulpicians, who are eminent in learning, but even more eminent in piety."[3]

McGivney, who was twenty-one when he arrived at St. Mary's in 1873, remained there for four years. Overall, his education stretched through nine years, over a patchwork of four schools (and two countries). In McGivney's case, however, nothing had fallen through the cracks—quite the opposite. Father Jean-Paul Gelinas observed in a 1961 profile of McGivney:

> Having received higher education and training under the diocesan priests of Sainte Hyacinthe Seminary in Quebec, the Vincentians of the Seminary of Our Lady of Angels in Niagara Falls, the Jesuits of Sainte-Marie College in Montreal, and under Sulpicians at Saint Mary's Seminary in Baltimore, Maryland, having the benefit of American and French culture added to his Irish background, the silent, determined and pious Michael Joseph McGivney was well prepared to be ordained a secular priest.[4]

McGivney emerged from school with a worldliness and an ability to see situations from a host of perspectives. Without hauteur, he had an aura of strength derived from the wide variety of people he had met in his studies and the situations he had mastered. In the tragic early death of his father, Mc-Givney walked for a terrible summer in the uncertain steps of those poor and troubled people he so boldly sought to assist through his vocation. Bereft even temporarily of the security and order that previously marked his life, he was tempered for the work before him.

For McGivney, one benefit of attaching his future to the Hartford Diocese was that he could be assured that he would always be near Waterbury. No outpost in the small state of Connecticut was more than a three-hour train ride from his hometown, so he could look forward to helping his family at last, in concrete ways. On the verge of becoming a priest, he made no secret of the fact that his fondest wish was that his two young brothers, John and Patrick, would hear the call from God as well. For the time being, it was a little hard to tell: neither of them was yet ten years old.

On December 22, 1877, in ceremonies at Baltimore's Cathedral of the Assumption, dozens of students from St. Mary's Seminary were promoted to various orders, or levels, in the path toward the priesthood: tonsure, minor orders, sub-deaconate, and deaconate. Over the previous three years, Michael Joseph McGivney had passed through each stage in turn. In that yuletide ceremony of 1877, he was ordained to the holy priesthood by Archbishop James Gibbons.

"What is the present condition of the Church?" Gibbons had sermonized only the year before at the consecration of the cathedral, referring to the state of American Catholicism. "We count sixty-seven Bishops, upwards of five thousand priests, six thousand five hundred churches, one thousand seven hundred Parish schools, with an aggregate attendance of nearly half a million of pupils, and a Catholic population exceeding six millions."

That was the state of the Church in the present tense, but for a new priest, Gibbons's message would continue, "what has already been done, gives us a hopeful assurance of what will be accomplished in the future, if we are only faithful in walking in the footsteps of our sires. The Providence of God has signally aided us in the past, by wafting emigrants to our shores. It is for us now to co-operate with heaven by building up the walls of Sion [Zion] whose broad foundations have been laid by our fathers."[5]

The challenge of drawing those wafts of new immigrants into the American Church was very real in the late 1870s— but so was the underlying anti-Catholic prejudice left over in the United States from the 1840s and 1850s. The two forces devolved directly onto the shoulders of a new priest, such as Michael McGivney. There were many in the Catholic clergy, veteran priests as well as bishops, who believed that the Church should merely steer its ancient, European-tinted course and that true believers would adhere to it. While that made for a quiet Church, it did not address the emerging problems of the era. Eventually, the Church would have to blend into American life and cater to its peculiar insecurities. How that might be accomplished was the concern that would define priests and the priesthood in Michael McGivney's coming age.

Although McGivney was ordained in Baltimore, his public debut as a priest came in Waterbury on Christmas Day, when he celebrated his first solemn Mass before friends and many relatives at his boyhood church, Immaculate Conception. The McGivney family would not know many Christmases that were more joyous. Michael himself could not have had a more exciting start to the new year of 1878, for he had been named curate in St. Mary's parish in New Haven.[6] The assignment, handed down by the new bishop of Hartford, Reverend Thomas Galberry, was a choice one, placing McGivney in a splendid, if impecunious, church.

The pastor was Father Patrick Murphy, an Irishman who had also completed his education at St. Mary's in Baltimore. He had received the second-highest marks ever recorded at the school, and was regarded as the finest classical scholar in the Hartford Diocese, studying ancient texts for several hours each day.[7] Murphy's health, however, was failing, and Bishop Galberry felt that the energetic, newly ordained Father McGivney would ease some of the burden. From that scenario, one might surmise that Father Murphy was a wizened old creature, hobbling around St. Mary's in his black robes, but in fact, he was only thirty-two.

When Father Murphy first arrived at St. Mary's in 1872 at the age of twenty-seven, he was a boy wonder . . . and the church was little more than a construction site. So it was that the diocese looked to him to complete the building, which had proved too much for its founding pastor after he started work on it two years earlier. St. Mary's was planned as a sumptuous structure, a jewel among Connecticut churches. No one doubted that, but people did wonder whether it would ever be finished. Then Father Murphy took charge. He oversaw the final construction, and presided over St. Mary's after its consecration in 1874. The effort was a ringing success, except inasmuch as it left St. Mary's with over $200,000 in debts, and Father Murphy with only a shadow of his former robust health. At one time, people in the diocese had talked about him as a future bishop; in 1878, they were only praying that he would stay alive.

Father McGivney immediately assumed responsibility for the daily operation of St. Mary's. Despite the beautiful edifice, it was one of the smaller parishes in the city, at least in terms of the number of worshippers. Among Father McGivney's underlying missions were building attendance and reducing the debt.

By comparison, Father Jeremiah Fitzpatrick of St. Patrick's Church, another Catholic parish in New Haven, labored with a debt of only $67,000—a great fortune in 1878, but not an entirely absurd one, like that of St. Mary's. Moreover, with his parish rolls full, he managed to lower the outstanding balance by about $30,000 each year.[8] Father Fitzpatrick was more than just beloved by his parishioners; he enjoyed a blend of respect and sheer adoration. A few years later, when he left for a vacation in Ireland, more than a thousand people bade him good-bye at the station; on his return, an even larger procession escorted his carriage back to St. Patrick's, stopping traffic all along the way.

In the realm of New Haven priests, however, the most celebrated was Father Hugh Carmody, pastor of St. John's Church. Whenever Church officials from the diocese or beyond visited the city, Dr. Carmody (the title he typically used) was the host. Tall, thin, and graceful, he "attracted attention as he walked through the streets to the post-office, by a bearing of some hauteur," wrote a contemporary, "through which could plainly be seen the intellectual force that could comprehend the various interests of life, in a way to enable him to treat generously men of almost every religious persuasion."[9] In other words, even Protestants were in awe of Dr. Carmody.

It might be said on the other hand that even Catholics were in awe of Dr. Edwin Harwood, the leading Episcopal minister in New Haven. Erudite and wealthy, Dr. Harwood was the rector of the Trinity Church, located on the Green and adjacent to the Yale University campus. A newspaper called the church "the most imposing in the city, perhaps in the state." Dr. Harwood was originally from Pennsylvania but reflected the members of New Haven's establishment of the 1870s exactly as they wished to see themselves: well-educated, fairly liberal in religious matters, and just a tad distant. Harwood lived with his large family at the rectory, where he liked best of all to escape into his study and into his books.[10]

The liberal religious climate of New Haven led to generally unstrained relations between the Catholic and Protestant communities—and between either one and the thriving Jewish population in the city. When Dr. Carmody complained that the history text assigned in the public high school contained bigoted statements regarding Catholics, the book may not have been withdrawn, but it was immediately designated as optional, rather than required, reading. The incident was symbolic of the peace that existed in cities like New Haven, where Catholics were tolerated quite gracefully, just as long as nothing occurred to disturb the accepted order.

New Haven had many, more pressing concerns, as Father McGivney found once he moved there. Manufacturing was vital, of course, as it was in nearly every town in southwestern Connecticut in the late nineteenth century. One factory in New Haven, so it was said, made five thousand different articles in various metals.[11] Many investors in the city were enthusiastic about the insurance business, which had practically exploded (if such a word can be used around an insurance company) in Hartford during the previous thirty years.

New Haven was ahead of other cities in developing the potential of the telephone, first demonstrated at the 1876 Centennial Exposition in Philadelphia. Only two years later, right after Father McGivney's arrival, a central switchboard was already changing life in the city. But first, residents had to understand it. "If a doctor wants his horse," explained the New Haven *Palladium,* "he 'calls' the central office, asks to be connected with the livery office, and when this is done, talks as freely with the livery man as though he had him face to face. In like manner, every person in the city who has a telephone can be connected with, and can converse with, every other person in the city who has one, no matter what the distance may be. Friends scattered around the city can 'call' each other and enjoy an evening's chat without leaving their firesides."[12]

Of all the burgeoning industries, though, it was still shipping that held the city in thrall. Three-masted schooners lined the wharves, and anyone with a little pocket change yearned to own a piece of an oceangoing ship: a quarter, a sixteenth, or even a thirty-second. Any news of a ship was a big story in New Haven.

With the new year, Father McGivney slipped quietly into the life of the city, into the Catholic community and St. Mary's Church. In mid-January, Bishop Galberry arrived at St. Mary's, ostensibly to confirm a large class of children and adults, but also to present a plan for expanding the parish, at the expense of others nearby. Father McGivney attended the confirmation, of course, and in late January performed his first marriage ceremony. A few weeks later, he attended a fund-raising fair sponsored by St. John's Church, and on February 10, he congregated with hundreds of priests from around the state at the dedication of Hartford's new cathedral. Actually, it was only the church basement that was being dedicated that day, but Bishop Galberry had been without any building of his own for more than two years and so it was still a major event.[13]

When Pope Pius IX died that month, Requiem Masses were held in every church; Father McGivney served as subdeacon in St. Mary's, with Father Murphy as the celebrant. St. Mary's pews were filled to an extent that might be termed respectful, but St. John's Church was filled to overflowing. Word had spread quickly through New Haven that Dr. Carmody had met the late pope—twice—and would speak about the experience in his eulogy.[14]

Dr. Carmody's reminiscences were reprinted verbatim in most of the New Haven papers, as he enthused over the "goodness" and "gentleness" of the departed pope. With his careful description of activity in the Vatican, he received a great deal of attention. That was more than some Protestants could stand, inspiring an offer from a group of six men, led by a sixty-two-year-old patent attorney named George Terry,[15] that they would pay the rent on a theater, if Dr. Carmody would enlarge upon his comments. Specifically, they asked him to respond to four points, including:

Is the institution known to the world as the Roman Catholic Church anything more or less than a feudal monarchy or government, Leo XIII [the new pope] at present being absolute monarch, priests being his officers, dioceses being the feuds or allotments of the chief feudatories, called bishops, *and a religion for the most part of their own making, being the means* by which they acquire their wealth and maintain their government?[16]

Dr. Carmody declined to answer the invitation. The younger priests in town watched as their old lion, unyielding in any fair fight, backed away and let the matter drop.

Only a few months out of school, Father McGivney could see all around him that it wasn't dangerous to be a Catholic in a modern city such as New Haven in the 1870s. But it wasn't easy, either.

6

IN CHARGE

"He had a soft, pleasant voice," a parishioner named Thomas Clark remembered of Father McGivney, "attracting attention by his perfect diction, which could also take a stern tone when necessary."[1]

Likewise, Reverend Daley recalled that "a blind, aged man who used to live by charity, but who was not a Catholic, went every Sunday to Mass at St. Mary's to hear 'that voice.' "[2] Even though some of Father McGivney's sermons generated comment in New Haven, none has survived in written form; only the echo of "that voice," as recalled by those who were drawn to it.

"He spoke slowly," Clark continued, "choosing precisely simple but emphatic words." Thomas Clark was five years old when the new curate arrived at St. Mary's in 1878. As a Sunday school student, he saw Father McGivney in class on a weekly basis. "Father McGivney was about five-foot-ten, slender," Clark said later, "giving the impression of being frail, although he never showed signs of illness."

"I saw him but once," admitted Father Daley, "and yet I remember his pale, beautiful face as if I saw it only yesterday; it was 'a priest's face,' and that explains everything, it was a face of wonderful repose; there was nothing harsh in that countenance although there was everything that was strong; there was nothing of the politician, nothing of the axe-grinder. Guile and ambition were as far from him as from heaven."[3]

Reverend W. J. Slocum, a priest who worked alongside McGivney in New Haven, called him "a man of unassuming character" in a 1905 talk, making the point that "he was almost childlike in his manner."[4] But there was another side.

Even while McGivney's face retained its innocence and calm, the way that he moved showed something just as important. "He ordinarily walked fast," Clark recalled. "Outside of the courses, he was serious, rather silent, methodic in his work; he held his head straight like a leader, his eyes very determined."

Most of the firsthand recollections of Father Michael McGivney make reference to that determination, that "strength of purpose" and "indomitable will." Other accounts of Father McGivney's appearance, however, contrast with the "serious, rather silent" countenance recalled by Thomas Clark. In photographs, McGivney's face did set itself into a sober, almost grim expression—and maybe that was typical for him, at least in repose. Or maybe, like most people, he had an image he wanted to project whenever his picture was taken and, like most, he tried a bit too hard to project it.

Around other people and in a natural setting, Father Mc-Givney was "light-hearted" and "pleasant," according to an unsigned profile written by an acquaintance in 1900. Over-flowing good humor was one of his three salient characteristics, according to his longtime friend Reverend Richard Foley of the Brooklyn Diocese (the other two being a deep sense of piety and orderliness). Over and over, contemporaries referred to his wit and the gentle way he could bring laughter into a room.

Perhaps the reason Thomas Clark thought that "outside of the courses," Father McGivney was so serious and silent betrays a small secret: every group thought itself particularly special in the eyes of the young priest. "To meet him was at once to trust him," observed Father Daley, "and the very old people of the neighborhood, whom he hunted up and who got part of his time even on busiest days, called him a positive saint and meant it." Women raising their families regarded him much the same way. Prisoners thought of him as their sincere friend; non–Catholics were uniquely attracted by his sympathetic quality.

Two groups were even more possessive around their priest than any of the others. The first consisted of the children of the parish. As the *Waterbury Democrat* expressed it, Father Mc-Givney "delighted in the companionship of children." Thomas Clark, along with other Sunday school children, could see that he was different around adults, and it struck him as serious and foreboding, at least by comparison to the personality they came to know as the head of the Sunday school.

"I never tired of him," Clark said in his recollection of Mc-Givney's teaching style. "His course on Catechism was well planned and he often used the children to personify characters of the Gospels. He spoke slowly, choosing precisely simple but emphatic words. He usually repeated the same explanation twice, rarely three times."

The second group with a special affinity for the new curate was composed of the teenagers in the parish. St. Mary's was not much different from other churches throughout the state, and the country, in watching many of them abandon their churchgoing habits. That was the problem. The young women in the sixteen-to-twenty-two-year-old range remained at least nominally attached to St. Mary's, but the young men dropped out in droves. One cause was a professed boredom with the church. The second, which followed almost automatically, was liquor. In many cases, that made the problem permanent.

As Father McGivney celebrated Mass during the first few months of 1878, he was no doubt inwardly thrilled to be performing the Church's most important ceremony and the Lord's work in general. But he was too sharp-eyed a man not to have his own joy tempered every time he looked out over the pews, where the ranks of the male parishioners were pathetically thin, except for the boys and the old men. St. Mary's looked like a church in wartime.

For all of the brooding problems of the Church in general, and the urgent ones of St. Mary's parishioners in particular, Father McGivney was fortunate to be living in a lively Catholic community. In New Haven, there was fun to be had, in the name of good works. During the gloom of late winter, St. John's Church sponsored its annual fund-raising fair, in much the usual manner for a Catholic church in the 1870s: renting a large hall and filling it with booths, concessions, and the contents of a veritable department store in the display for the prizes. Attendance at such fairs was a polite obligation for priests in adjoining parishes, and during the last week of February Father McGivney attended the St. John's fair with his pastor, Father Murphy. A few weeks later, when the fair ended, the raffle winners were announced. Father McGivney didn't win a thing but had to help Father Murphy carry home all his prizes: a pair of vases, a set of goblets, and a box of lace curtains.[5]

On March 17, Father Murphy finished the regular service with Father McGivney at the altar and then announced that, in honor of the day, a song called "St. Patrick's Day in the Morning" would be played on the organ. In his low voice, weakened by illness, he asked everyone to join in the singing. The parishioners were taken aback, never having heard secular music, and a winsome little ditty at that, ring out in their church before. The organist, Thomas Fitzgerald, had the sheet music ready, though, and, on cue, he struck up the first chords. "The choir and congregation—a very large one," noted an observer, "sang the popular Irish song with great effect, many being moved to tears."[6]

Father McGivney joined in the singing that morning, but in general, he steered clear of the more insistent celebrations of St. Patrick's Day, the big parades and banquets that spread green throughout New Haven. He took only a polite interest in the Land League movement, by which many churches, including St. Mary's, raised money to buy tracts in Ireland for displaced tenant farmers. Father McGivney didn't think of himself as an Irishman, not even a part-time one. His parents had brought him up as an American. That was how he regarded his parishioners, too, even the many who had been born in Kerry, Derry, or Donegal: Americans.

Father McGivney had another reason for staying away from St. Patrick's Day and the green-sashed men who drank endless toasts to it. He didn't much like the groups behind the celebrations. Some of them were little more than drinking cliques. No one needed to encourage them, least of all a parish priest who saw firsthand what drunkenness did to a man, and then to his family. In other cases, though, the Irish-American clubs fell into the category of "secret societies," with rituals, incantations, and signs known only to members. Secret societies were distracting at best—and sacrilegious when taken to their extreme. In any case, the Church had no use for them and specifically forbade Catholics to participate in secret rituals. For that reason, Father McGivney let the Ancient Order of Hibernians and the Knights of St. Patrick march downtown to their banquets without him.

For the same reason, Father McGivney was pained to read in the papers on Monday, May 27, that a group of churchgoing Catholics in New Haven were using two of the oldest secret societies as their model. "A Roman Catholic Mutual Burial Association, similar in design to the Masonic and Oddfellows organizations," read the report, "was formed last evening. . . . No restriction was placed on nationality as to membership, but members must belong to the Catholic church."[7] The need for mutual life (or burial) insurance was not at issue. The troubling aspect lay with the very need to belong that made many such societies successful. Devout believers derived their sense of belonging from the Church. Outside groups that offered a separate identity for Catholics and, likewise, demanded a separate and very deep-seated allegiance could not fit into their life. The new group in New Haven did not last past a second meeting, but the conundrum for Catholic men remained. They may have wanted to enter into a secret brotherhood, for those satisfying aspects of belonging, but they couldn't, according to their Church.

The following Sunday evening, Father McGivney was at a gathering that he considered much more promising: his first meeting of the St. Joseph's Young Men's Total Abstinence and Literary Society.[8]

Long before he arrived, he had to be given a quick tutorial on New Haven and its Total Abstinence (TA) societies. The first matter to clear up, was that St. Mary's TA society was called St. Joseph's; St. Patrick's was called St. Mary's; and St. John's was called St. Aloysius's. Only if Father McGivney could unravel all that and pick out the right saint would he end up at the right meeting on Sunday night. He did, meeting a small group of men in their late teens and early twenties who had "taken the pledge" not to drink alcoholic beverages.

Abstinence from liquor was the theme of TA societies throughout the nation, especially in the Northeast, where there was the greatest concentration of Irish-Americans. It might be tempting to think that the popularity of TA societies with the Irish was connected to the traditional and tragic Gaelic problem with alcohol—except that so many other nationalities have that same traditional and tragic problem. It is a fact that in the late nineteenth century, a large proportion of Irish-American men fell victim to alcoholism. In joining the

St. Joseph's Young Men's Total Abstinence and Literary (TAL) Society, Father McGivney was not merely performing another job expected of a church leader. He intended to find out why so many of his young parishioners became drunks, while others managed to avoid it.

In a typical TA society, coaxing young men into giving up liquor was the goal; a low-grade insurance plan was the lure. Known as Total Abstinence and Benevolent societies, organizations of that type acted as a kind of ongoing "sunshine fund." If something happened to a member or one of his close relatives, a small assessment would be gathered from each of the others in the group and delivered where needed. St. Joseph's, however, was not a benevolent society, in that sense. It may have been intrinsically benevolent, but it was officially a literary society, and in the churchly setting, that referred to anything regarded as a wholesome pursuit, from ball games to billiards. The main occupation of a successful TAL, however, was the production of plays. Theatricals kept the young men amused, challenged, confident, probably a little sweaty, and, it is to be hoped, sober. Plays also raised money.

Unfortunately, the St. Joseph's TAL Society was in no position to put on a play. It had been founded at St. Mary's in 1873, the year before the new church building was finished, but membership had never been robust. In fact, things were so dull in the little club that one of the most dedicated parishioners in St. Mary's Church, John McWeeney, drifted over to St. Patrick's Church and joined its TA (the one called St. Mary's), even serving as president. In June 1878, surrounded by the stragglers who still belonged to St. Joseph's TAL, Father McGivney allowed himself to be elected treasurer in what was supposed to be an effort at reorganization. He could have headed the TAL but instead chose to take a secondary role. That preference was typical of McGivney's thinking: as long as necessary, he would support the effort as a kind of backbone, but his ambition was for others to learn how to run the club.

All the members of St. Joseph's TAL were workingmen: John Rourke, twenty years old, the recording secretary, painted carriages for a living. Henry McDermott, twenty-six, the chairman of the board of directors, was a bricklayer. Joseph Miller, twenty-three, who would work closely with Father McGivney as the financial secretary, earned his keep by helping out in his family's music store, or "melodian shop."[9] For the time being, with new momentum only just beginning, the dozen members of the TAL sipped on soft drinks in the basement of St. Mary's and told Father McGivney in great detail what kind of club rooms they would like to have someday. (Over at St. Aloysius's Total Abstinence and Benevolent Society, which Dr. Carmody had founded for the youth at St. John's, the fellows had their own lounge in a downtown office building.)[10]

Even as the weather grew more mild in late spring, Father Murphy's health grew weaker. He was diagnosed with tuberculosis, the scourge of the nineteenth century. Although the disease was not always fatal, it ravaged the crowded immigrant neighborhoods of America's cities—and the parish priests who visited them or worked within them.

Looking drawn and gray, Father Murphy performed as

many of his duties as possible but continued to leave the bulk of his responsibilities at St. Mary's to Father McGivney. On Thursday, June 27, the two priests were at the rectory when someone arrived with the message that Father Murphy's presence would be very desirable in the basement of the church. Perplexed, he left immediately. He was accompanied by Father McGivney, who pretended to be just as bewildered.

The basement meeting room was crowded with members of the Young Ladies' and Girls' sodalities, eager to make a presentation. Though McGivney had been at St. Mary's barely half a year, he had worked regularly with the sodalities and knew all of the many parishioners awaiting Father Murphy. The young ladies went first. After an address of appreciation by a prim and slightly nervous emissary of the group, Mary Downes (a daughter of Edward Sr., the stationer) stepped forward. She handed Father Murphy a basket of flowers, "in the midst of which, and enclosed in a nutshell, was a check for $125." The idea behind the June gift was that Father Murphy would make use of the money when he took a summer vacation. The children had their turn next; their representative stepped forward and said that "though they were little girls, they loved and respected their pastor as well as their elder sisters." In their basket of flowers was a nutshell containing a check for $75. Proportionately, that was a great deal of money from the little ones. Father Murphy thanked them all gently and asked for their prayers, even as he bestowed his blessing on the beaming faces before him.[11]

The summer had hardly begun before it turned frighteningly hot. In late June, a worker in the nearby town of New Britain died of sunstroke. The word was that he had once lived in South Africa, where he toiled in temperatures of 110, but Connecticut's particularly stifling air killed him.[12] Residents of New Haven talked of little else except the hot temperatures, because, according to the weather reports, even higher ones were on the way from the Midwest, where hundreds had died from the heat. Fear brought on some bizarre trends in fashion. People walked around New Haven in wet clothes, and staid businessmen put leaves in their hats in order to absorb some of the heat. "No precautions were omitted that might avert a possibly fatal sickness," reported a local newspaper. Nonetheless, New Haveners were dropping in the streets, either from the 90-degree temperatures or from terror over the worse weather on the way. "The sun was angry looking," reported the *Evening Register,* "and the air dull and depressing, and there seemed to be reason enough for gloomy foreboding."[13]

By July 7, Father Murphy had had all that he could take of the angry sun. With his own money—and that which he had received from the sodalities, he didn't have to remain in the city. Until his respiratory condition eased, it would be dangerous even to try. He announced after Mass that Sunday that he was compelled to leave St. Mary's for five or six weeks, as a reporter noted, "on account of his health being very poor." Father Murphy planned to visit Saratoga Springs in upstate New York. Most people in the congregation were saddened, but at the same time relieved to think that the pastor was going to escape the treacherous heat. The members of the Scapular and Rosary Society, however, were taken entirely by surprise. Rushing to organize an impromptu meeting after the service, they collected $200 to give Father Murphy.[14] While the grown-

ups scrambled, their little girls watched, having taken care of
their own business with the pastor with perfect aplomb, a week
and a half before.

On Tuesday, July 9, Father Murphy started on his vacation, leaving Father McGivney to preside over St. Mary's
alone.[15] It was quite a load for a man just six months out of
seminary. Father McGivney's plight, however, didn't stay in
the news for long. The very next day, New Haven's Catholic
community was rocked with an even bigger story: Dr. Carmody was leaving, having been transferred to a pastorate in
the town of New Britain. On Wednesday, his parishioners
heard the news, and on Thursday, Carmody was gone. All that
was left in his wake were the sobs of parishioners and fruitless
entreaties made to the bishop to reverse the decision.[16] Father
Carmody had been a strong influence on Michael McGivney,
who was among the many who were sorry to see him go. The
imperturbable dignity of the older priest was a lesson for a
new man who hoped to be as successful in his parish as Father
Carmody had been at St. John's.

Father McGivney was so busy at his church that for
months he neglected to write to one of his favorite professors,
Father Alphonse Magnien, who had taken over as head of Mc-
Givney's alma mater earlier in the year. "It is with a deep sense
of confusion that I at this late hour think of congratulating
you on your promotion to the Superiorship of St. Mary's
Seminary," McGivney began. "But I know your kind heart
will overlook the delay & forgive one when you know that I
have been alone all Summer with the whole work of a parish
on my shoulders. I have not had time for even one day's vacation since I left St. Mary's. . . . So pardon me the delay."[17]

While Father Murphy was away in Saratoga Springs, Father McGivney did more than merely keep St. Mary's Church open. He did, of course, conduct all of the services, which were less demanding than usual, inasmuch as sermons were not preached in any of the Catholic churches during July and August. He celebrated a handful of baptisms and one wedding, and he handled one rather sad crisis. On the last day of July, Thomas Fitzgerald, the organist at St. Mary's, suddenly quit, distraught over family problems stemming from the death of a child some time before. Father McGivney couldn't reach him because the musician had, in his distress, rushed to New York City. His condition deteriorated there and he was committed to an insane asylum.[18] In Fitzgerald's absence, Father McGivney turned to Josephine Downes, from the devout family of stationers, engaging her to play the organ.

Father McGivney was also in charge of the annual church picnic. While that may sound like a quaint little occupation, in the case of St. Mary's, thousands of people were expected to attend the outing. Some parish priests in the 1870s still disdained the very idea of a picnic, claiming that no good could come from people mixing in such a liberal way.[19] Father McGivney, however, was not one of them. As had Father Rice at Niagara, he loved to see people having fun within the embrace of the Church. McGivney not only oversaw the plans for the picnic—in his meticulous way, he embellished them at every turn. Well in advance, he scheduled a baseball game, dividing the volunteers between an "uptown" team and a "downtown" team. He also arranged for a horse race at the picnic grounds and special horse-drawn cars to transport children to the park.[20]

The newspapers did not report the finish of the horse race, but they did marvel at the many new features of the picnic: the pleasures, the amusements, the overall enjoyment. Perhaps it wasn't much, just a church picnic on a sunny August day in New Haven. But it was the best that it could have been. That capsule was at the core of a reputation that Father McGivney was already building in what ought to have been an overwhelming summer, his first as a priest.

The uptowns won the game, 14–4.

7

A CHURCH FAIR

Of the six Catholic parishes located in New Haven in the 1870s, St. Mary's was the second smallest, with about 2500 communicants. That was a fairly low number, compared with the 4500 who were attached to St. John's, where Dr. Carmody had been pastor, and the 6000 who looked to Father Fitzpatrick at St. Patrick's Church.[1] St. Mary's did, however, draw a certain added strength from its location on Hillhouse Avenue, in the heart of New Haven's most upstanding neighborhood. The reputation enjoyed by the street was all part of the plan of the Honorable James Hillhouse, the former senator who laid it out seventy years before—and the man who planted the first elm trees in the self-proclaimed Elm City.

Throughout the nineteenth century, a drive up Hillhouse Avenue was *de rigueur* for tourists. For their benefit, hack drivers entered the street ringing out with "This street is occupied by the literary aristocracy of New Haven!" or "Here live rich widows from Boston!"[2] The truth lay somewhere in between. Bankers and factory owners moved in and out of the huge houses of Hillhouse Avenue with each passing generation, and so did Yale professors, including those with names still venerated today: Silliman, Kingsley, Sheffield, and Dana.

With the towers of Yale University overlooking Hillhouse Avenue, news of the school drifted inevitably into St. Mary's sanctuary. In January 1879, the latest campus scandal shot unexpectedly out of a minstrel show put on by a group of freshmen. A minstrel show was a musicale in which white performers wore blackface, in keeping with an imitation of the uniquely exuberant style of singing originated by African-Americans in the South. Rejected as disrespectful during the twentieth century, minstrel shows were regarded as low-grade entertainment even at the height of their popularity in the last half of the nineteenth century. The Yale freshmen, at any rate, thought it was terrific fun. "The minstrel show was preceded by a play and was the first entertainment, I believe, that any of the Freshmen societies had given to the University for some time," recalled Dick Bissell, a member of the Yale class of 1883 and a performer in the troupe. "The consensus of opinion seemed to be that the performers had disgraced themselves and there was considerable excitement on the Campus the next morning, Sunday, as a result of our performance."

Somewhere in the midst of the freshman debacle was David Hillhouse Buel, a distant relative of the late James Hillhouse. While studying at Yale, he was staying with an uncle, William Hillhouse, whose house was next door to St. Mary's

Church. Buel's pedigree matched or bettered that of anyone on the street: his first American ancestor arrived in 1630. His grandfather (Williams College '33) had been a Congregational minister, and his father, a Union officer in the Civil War. At Yale, Ted Buel, as he was known, was interested in theater, especially the writing part of it, and he was one of the principal authors of the freshman show.

"I was persuaded to go to a prayer meeting after chapel," Dick Bissell continued, speaking of that unexpectedly steamy winter weekend, "and was made extremely uncomfortable by the impassioned address of a Senior who advised the members of the Freshman class to ostracize the men who, by their frivolous and ribald behavior in the show the night before, had brought disgrace to the class. Until the night before I had been rather proud of the fact that I was a member of the minstrel troupe; but my self-esteem was very rudely shocked at the prayer meeting."[3]

After the obligatory chapel services at Yale, Ted Buel had taken to attending Mass at St. Mary's. Buel discovered a good friend in Father McGivney, who did not disparage his interest in writing for the theater. In the wake of the minstrel show fracas, though, the priest did encourage Buel away from the rocky laughs of burlesque toward a more lasting kind of wit. Buel turned to the classics, in the style of Gilbert and Sullivan, and began work on his next oeuvre, *Medea: A Travesty*.

Ted Buel was one of a number of Protestants who attended St. Mary's Church regularly. Some were unabashedly there to hear the choir, choosing their seats only for sake of the acoustics.[4] Others were drawn to that particular church by the two priests, each one intriguing in his own way: the fading brilliance of Father Murphy and the innate optimism of Father McGivney.

Nevertheless, the church still irritated a great many Protestants on Hillhouse Avenue. They wondered how such a well-planned stronghold of old money had become host to the "immigrant church." To Father Edward J. O'Brien, the pastor who started building St. Mary's in 1870, that was exactly the point: he wanted to wipe away the image of the Catholic Church as a second-class institution. Admittedly, good Father O'Brien should never have been allowed anywhere near a checkbook during the planning of the new church in New Haven. The debt he incurred drove him to a nervous breakdown, followed by a state of semiretirement in a much smaller parish. Nonetheless, his spirit of unbounded ambition for American Catholics was both well timed and well placed.

Mary O'Brien Driscoll, Father O'Brien's niece, was among the first people whom Father McGivney met in New Haven. She and her family had remained in the parish, where they were compelled by the same impatient O'Brien blood. But not even an O'Brien could match Mary's new husband, Cornelius Driscoll, in his drive toward the center of American success, and his determination to belong there.

Cornelius Driscoll had been born in County Kerry in southwestern Ireland, arriving in America as a young boy in about 1850. He and his parents settled on a farm in the eastern Connecticut town of Norwich. At the Free Academy there, Driscoll studied hard in a college prep course, blithely ignoring the fact that Irish Catholics were unknown and unwelcome at most American colleges. As the Civil War ended, however, the door to higher education opened a crack, and when it did, Driscoll was ready to slip through. He entered Yale University in 1865, cutting expenses by staying with an uncle, Patrick McKiernan, in New Haven. Driscoll graduated from Yale in 1869 and took a degree at the law school two years later.[5] At the time, he was the only Catholic in the Yale Law School.

Cornelius Driscoll was a man of medium build with straight features and thinning brown hair. His success was derived less from any charisma that he exuded than from his ability to drive good ideas through to completion. In his first year of law school, he had recruited five other men to help him start America's first statewide Catholic Temperance Union.[6] Out of his group grew the National Catholic Temperance Union, which was an active force for the next forty years.

As Driscoll launched his career, he was the second Catholic lawyer ever to practice in the city of New Haven, the first having been Edward Downes Sr.'s older brother, William. In January 1879, Driscoll was also starting a long flirtation with politics, taking a seat as a newly elected city alderman. Father McGivney, working tirelessly to establish St. Joseph's TAL, was impressed by Cornelius Driscoll, who was, at thirty-four, the grand old man of Catholic temperance unions. The brilliant Driscoll, for his part, recognized that McGivney was a natural leader, and the two formed a close bond. Each was hoping to help younger Catholic men fulfill their potential in a country still riddled with prejudice against them: Driscoll by pulling from the front of the pack, with McGivney watching over the back, allowing no stragglers. Leading from the back was the style of a parish priest—it was by no means easy, but it suited McGivney perfectly.

On the last Sunday in January 1879, Father McGivney served as subdeacon at St. Mary's while the bishop-elect of the Hartford Diocese, Lawrence McMahon, administered confirmation to approximately 200 children and adults.[7] McMahon had replaced Bishop Galberry, who died suddenly after only two years in the bishopric. Although McMahon had a fine intellect, he bore the husky, rough-hewn appearance of a lumberjack or a fisherman. Some of that was borne out in his personality as well. McMahon was indeed tough, more respected than beloved in the parishes in which he had served. He met Father Michael McGivney for the first time at the confirmation, forming a positive opinion that would last throughout his own long bishopric and affect them both.

The one man who was not present at the confirmation was Father Murphy. With only one lung functioning, he was on yet another short vacation in hopes of regaining his old vigor.[8] His place at the St. Mary's confirmation ceremony was taken by Father Patrick Lawlor of New London, Connecticut. Lawlor certainly knew Father McGivney: the two were brothers-in-law, Mary McGivney having married Michael Lawlor back in Waterbury.

Father Lawlor was a self-contained man, not wasting much of his charm (if indeed he had any) on the people around him. But he had executive ability: the most recent of his triumphs was the resuscitation of a flagging parish in New London into one of the most robust in the diocese. A few weeks after he returned to New London from New Haven, he showed his stern

stuff by announcing at Sunday services that henceforth he
would publicly announce the names of all Catholics who appeared in criminal court, making sure to describe the accusa-
tions against them to the entire congregation.[9]

Even when Father Murphy wasn't away, seeking rest,
nearly all of the responsibility of running St. Mary's Church
fell to Father McGivney. Father McGivney took a long perspective, though, in the way that he saw the parish. For that
reason, he gladly devoted all of the time demanded by the St.
Joseph's TAL. Anytime he was called by the parents of a
brawling teenager or asked to intervene when a young man
was fired from a job for drunkenness, he thought of the TAL
and the hope it offered men for surviving and enjoying the
most treacherous period in their lives.

"The Society was organized a little over a year ago," the
Connecticut Catholic reported in mid-1879, "but is now one of
the largest of the kind in the State, having a membership of
over 100, and is constantly increasing, which is mainly due to
the efforts of Rev. Fr. McGivney."[10] In March, the society decided to use its newfound muscle to stage a theatrical production for St. Patrick's Day. McGivney, keeping to his role as
Treasurer, did not choose the play—*Handy Andy*—or schedule
the performance on the holiday. He did give the initial go-
ahead, though, and oversaw the expenses, which were considerable, since the group decided to go for broke by renting a
professional theater called the Music Hall for the gala night.
At least, they hoped it would be a bit gala.

The part of Handy Andy was played by twenty-three-year-
old Joe Hines, born in England of Irish parents and employed
as a common laborer. James Kinlan, a twenty-two-year-old

machinist, played Mr. Purlong, an English fop. John Hopkins, a tailor who was twenty-two, was Squire O'Grady. Thomas P. Harrison, a helper in a piano shop at the age of sixteen, played one of the villains. As March 17 approached, the dozen or so men in the cast rehearsed under the direction of Billy Homer, one of the TAL members, who was described as "one long accustomed to the business of the stage."[11] He was twenty-three. Father McGivney stood by, in the form of an executive producer. When the curtain rose, the theater was full.

The major New York papers neglected to send their theater critics. In fact, so did the local New Haven papers. But the *Connecticut Catholic* did come through with a review of *Handy Andy*. For regular readers, the level of criticism in the *Connecticut Catholic* was best measured by the length of the review. Always kind, the weekly newspaper simply noted the flops, but it devoted endless space to the hits. Therefore, it may have made the star comedian flush with pride to read that "Handy Andy (Joe Hines), who never did a thing without blunder, was the life of the play," but the proof that a new era was dawning for the St. Joseph's TAL lay in the fact that the review took up almost a whole column. "This is the first dramatic entertainment which the young men of this society have given," the review explained near the top, "and it reflects great credit both on the history of the society and the abilities of Billy Homer."[12]

Handy Andy netted three hundred dollars for the society, which soon had a beautiful set of rooms on Church Street downtown, supplied with a library of books, current magazines, and newspapers. A piano was soon added, along with a walking path on the lawns adjoining.

For a parish priest, used to working with individuals and counting successes one by one, the smash hit at the Music Hall was heady stuff. Not that Father McGivney was suddenly stagestruck but, rather, he was able to see all at once the good that a Catholic group such as the TAL could render in the lives of dozens, if not hundreds, of men. They were attached to the Church in a more dynamic way than before, while relying on mutual support to resist common temptations (notably liquor). And they were engaged in a positive activity—in the case of *Handy Andy*, learning the art of slapstick. All of that was more than just all right with Father McGivney, even the slapstick. He was barely one year out of seminary, and he was deeply impressed by the TAL's explosive growth, his first success on a wide scale.

While every era believes itself to be in the vanguard of scientific improvement, new inventions were changing life in New Haven, even over the short span of time that Father McGivney had been at St. Mary's. One year after the city became the first in the world to try out a telephone exchange, the company that pioneered it had sixty miles of cable reaching all neighborhoods. "The telephone," observed the *New Haven Evening Register,* "has become of prime necessity." That was the year that was, but the one coming promised even more changes. In early 1879, New Haven depended on gaslight, with 882 street lamps illuminating the city. Gas was also in most homes and nearly every business. That was about to change, with the installation of the first electric lights in the Willamantic Linen Company. The 72 gas lamps that lit the factory's mule room, measuring 200 by 70 feet, were replaced by just 4 electric lights.[13]

Exciting things were happening in the city of New Haven and at St. Mary's Church, in particular, but Father Murphy could not enjoy any of it. In early spring, he decided to go to Europe for a complete rest. He even booked passage from Edward Downes Sr.,[14] who had started a sideline in selling steamship tickets. Sadly, the session Father Murphy spent with Downes planning the trip was a kind of high point. His respiratory condition declined from then on, and in May, his mother arrived from nearby Bridgeport to stay near him. By then, it was apparent that Murphy's chronic tuberculosis had given way to typhoid malaria, an even more virulent disease that racked his weakened body. Father McGivney assumed all of the priestly duties at St. Mary's, as he had many times before, but spent as much time as he could with Father Murphy. Other priests also paid long visits to the rectory. During the week of May 12, Murphy's condition turned critical, as he drifted out of consciousness. In all six Catholic churches in New Haven, special prayers were offered for his sake on May 18.[15]

That afternoon, the prayers were answered. Father Murphy woke up and gave his physician hope of a recovery. In the evening, the priest chatted with the many family members who had joined Father McGivney and other local priests at his bedside.

The next day, Father Murphy could no longer recognize Father McGivney or anyone else. He died in the afternoon. Almost a hundred priests attended his funeral two days later. Remarkably, Father McGivney had no official role in the funeral. He was no doubt busy in the background, working to manage the details. But he had been overlooked as others took part in the obsequies. Still, Father McGivney wanted to make an even fuller contribution in honor of his good friend, and led a committee to place a tablet at the church in memory of Father Murphy. It was perhaps the only example of a situation in which Father McGivney rather insistently made all of the decisions. The result was a set of two memorial stones still visible at the church, one inside and one set into a wall on the outside.

For more than a month, Father McGivney was acting pastor of St. Mary's. Although he did an impeccable job, he couldn't be appointed permanent pastor; one year out of seminary, he lacked the requisite experience. On the other hand, no else wanted the job. With financial problems perennially hanging over the parish, several priests who were asked to take St. Mary's responded by asking to be excused from the assignment. Father Lawlor, in New London, was asked twice and demurred. Finally, on June 19, the diocese announced that the new pastor would be . . . Father Patrick Lawlor, who had acquiesced on the third request. There were those in the diocese who regarded his decision to take on the killing debt of St. Mary's as nothing short of heroic.

Father Lawlor had barely learned his way around the rectory in late July, when St. Mary's received a blow from an unexpected source. *The New York Times,* seemingly prodded by one of the church's unmollified neighbors on Hillhouse Avenue, published a long article titled "An Unprofitable Church: How an Aristocratic Avenue was Blemished by a Roman Church Edifice." The tone was openly, even gratuitously anti-Catholic, describing the negotiations leading to the selection of the lot and implying that St. Mary's was built on Hillhouse Avenue solely to spite New Haven's leading Protestants. It concluded by saying that the church "is an eye-sore on the avenue, a source of annoyance and injury to neighboring residents and a complete failure as a business enterprise."[16] With a bit of research, *The New York Times* could have learned that St. Mary's Church was not actually intended as a business enterprise. In any case, the article received tremendous attention, with its placement at the top of page one. Throughout, it questioned the Catholics' wisdom in spending so much money on a church building, and even insinuated that the parish might soon renege on its debts. In addition to causing a whirlpool of concern in St. Mary's parish—and in New Haven banking circles—the article succeeded in expanding the church's notoriety as an example of Catholic excess. The next day, the *New Haven Morning Journal and Courier* leaped to its defense, calling it "the fine church on Hillhouse Avenue" and bristling at the idea that it might cheat anyone out of so much as a dollar, let alone $165,000 of them.[17]

Father McGivney left the issues of finance to Father Lawlor, a man who was just as sharp as any of the bankers or accountants with whom he dealt on a weekly or even daily basis. As a means of showing a strong face in the aftermath of the *New York Times* article, both priests attended the St. John's Church parish picnic at Hamilton Park on Wednesday, July 30. Their very presence, looking relaxed and taking some sun, was an open indication that St. Mary's was all right and unashamed.

At least, the parish was unashamed until the sporting events started. Father McGivney stepped up to participate in a shooting match with several other priests. Despite being a very good marksman, he didn't win. And neither did his baseball team: St. Joseph's TAL lost to St. Aloysius's TAB, 5–2.

Near the bandstand, an even more disturbing situation was unfolding, as a young man named Thomas Lahey had an argument with one of his erstwhile friends, a fellow named Shea. Either they were bickering about the girl with whom Shea was dancing, or they were just bickering from beer and excitement. On the verge of a fistfight, they were separated, but only temporarily. After Shea left Hamilton Park, Lahey jumped him. A few other men came along and tried to stop the fight, but even so it escalated. As Lahey and Shea rolled on the ground in what one of the witnesses called "deadly combat," the others looked around the streets in vain for a policeman.

Bystanders tried and failed to separate the two men, but Lahey and Shea were in a real dogfight. "Shea was trying to bite Lahey's ear off," a witness said.

At that moment, Father McGivney came upon the fight, drawn by the shouting. His mere presence, standing over the two grapplers, distracted Shea, who stopped trying to bite Lahey's ear. Lahey noticed McGivney then, too, and let go of Shea. Even in the heat of the moment, McGivney took charge and "told the men to shake hands and make up," the witnesses related, "and Shea shook hands as requested."[18]

Not that baseball and amateur theatricals solved all of the problems of the world, but breaking up fights such as that between Lahey and Shea—and there were others—made Father McGivney all the more determined to give the Catholic men in his charge more options in their daily lives, and a better perspective on how they looked at themselves. The Church offered a wealth of answers for their needs, but in the first place, something very real in the modern era had to hold them to the Church. He continued to work on that problem. He also turned his attention to something a little less important, at least in the long run.

A week after St. John's picnic, St. Mary's parish had its own outing. All the New Haven priests were in attendance and, once again, Father McGivney allowed himself to be entered in the shooting contest. He made the high score and took the whole match.

Meanwhile, St. Joseph's TAL may have lost its second ball game in as many weeks to St. Aloysius's TAB, but the society was busy practically all of the time, taking in new pledges and planning more events. In July, it chartered a boat to Long Island, about an hour's trip across the Sound, with all of the priests in the city along as guests, as were the orphans from the local Catholic asylum. In August, the society staged an evening of poetry recitals and singing for invited guests. It was such a rousing success that they repeated the format two weeks later.[19]

In the autumn, while Father Lawlor negotiated with St. Mary's creditors, Father McGivney was left with the chore of trying to raise funds. People from other parishes were beginning to complain publicly that St. Mary's debt was on the verge of ruining all of the Catholic churches in New Haven. Any parish priest has to have a bit of the entrepreneur in him, but in November, McGivney came up with a new machine for pulling coins out of willing comers. It was a "coffee festival," a novelty that combined one part coffee—always a high-profit item—with desserts and a bit of entertainment. Under Mc-Givney's direction, the women of the parish joined forces with his loyal troops from the TAL to open the coffee festival. Someone connected with the effort made a stab at an advertisement for the newspaper, another first for a church fund-raiser in New Haven:

> Well! Well! Didn't you hear the latest? Why, they are going to have a Coffee Party in the Church street Hall next Thursday night. Yes, and they are going to have lots of fun, too! At least so the ladies say. All kinds of party games, music, dancing etc. The members of St. Joseph's Young Men's Society will contribute to the success of the evening's enjoyment by introducing character sketches, songs, dances, etc. The party promises to be as enjoyable as its name is original.[20]

Father McGivney could not miss any chance to bring in funds.[21] Sometime in between celebrating Mass eight or ten times per week and hearing confessions, performing baptisms, and counseling the weak and troubled—those things that he was taught to do in seminary—he opened a swinging nightspot in downtown New Haven.

The coffee festival was supposed to run only one night, but because of the overwhelming attendance, it stayed open a week. It could have remained open indefinitely, as a going business, but Father McGivney did have to sleep at some point. "Father McGivney deserves great credit for the way he conducted it," marveled one account. "It is reported that he netted quite a nice sum, which will help to pay off the debt on the church property."

That was the quest that never lifted from the minds of the priests at St. Mary's.

8

MODERN MEN

Sometime in late 1878 or early 1879, Cornelius Driscoll introduced one of his new friends in politics, James T. Mullen, to Father McGivney. A communicant of St. Patrick's Church, Mullen had already heard a great deal about the energetic priest across town at St. Mary's. And Father McGivney had no doubt heard something about James T. Mullen.

Driscoll and Mullen had lived very different lives, yet both had arrived at nearly the same position. They were the ones to watch in New Haven, at the vanguard of the first generation of Irish Catholics to assert their ambitions publicly. Mullen, who would turn thirty-six in 1880, had not had any of the educational opportunities granted to—or grasped by—Cornelius Driscoll. Born in New Haven, he had gone to public schools with no thought of college afterward. He enlisted in the Union army during the Civil War and served about a year and a half in Company C of the Ninth Connecticut Volunteers before he was discharged on account of illness. Once he recovered, he became a policeman in New Haven. A little later, he entered the world of business as a liquor dealer.[1]

Mullen stood five foot seven and weighed a hefty 220 pounds. His features were quite ordinary, with his shallow eyes and fleshy nose. Yet he managed to draw attention to himself with a handlebar moustache that was extravagant, even in an era that made a contest of men's facial hair. Mullen was a tireless man, with a personality that was quite the opposite of Driscoll's carefully measured manner. Mullen would work a crowd, while Driscoll would merely survey it. In the drive to succeed, however, the two were well matched. Mullen was making his way up on the basis of connections; and if he didn't have them, he made them. Every era offers opportunities to such go-getters, but the post–Civil War years were especially fertile for a person who could remember names—and then do something with them.

After the war ended, many veterans, particularly in the victorious North, were loath to leave the army entirely behind. They didn't mind consigning the grisly scenes of battle to the past, but the camaraderie of camp life was something that veterans still craved. To keep the old troops together, they formed honor guards and quasi-military organizations. Some groups, like New Haven's Sarsfield Guard, also admitted new recruits, inculcating them to army life, or least the part of it that might echo through a prosperous New England city. The Sarsfield

Guard was filled with Irish-Americans, including James Mullen, who gladly put on the bright red uniform and worked his way up in the new ranks.

While the troops of the Sarsfield Guard were practicing their drills and spending summer weekends a-tenting, other men in the United States were just as restless to redefine the image that they saw in the mirror each day. They were the dutiful American men of the Gilded Age, that time of conspicuous growth in the late 1800s. The era was by no means named for them. It was named for the gold-tinged way of life of those industrial and financial titans who were taking over the economy, if not the whole country. If workingmen were just along for the ride, then more and more, they were the ones in the harnesses.

For the majority of men, working for someone else was something new. Their fathers and grandfathers had been adventurers on an individual scale, running their own farms or their own one-man shops or engaging in another kind of work that may not have made them rich but did make them the masters of their own days. Or they were adventurers on a grander scale: immigrants, finding a new place in the world. Or pioneers, cutting down trees and taking their food off the land. For the men living in America's big cities and factory towns in the Gilded Age, the adventures of their fathers were only a fading memory. In the new manner of manhood thrust upon them, the decisions of the day were no longer theirs. They were told what to do, and when, and even why—that is, how much they would be paid.

Of course, they received a measure of stability unknown to their fathers. But it was a large dose to gulp all at once. A man starting in the factories at twenty in 1880 could pretty well predict just where he would be at sixty in 1920. If he was still alive, he would be working in a factory, possibly the same one, and living on the same street, probably in the same house. The satisfaction of building upon something and gaining a new life through it was left to his fathers and his grandfathers.

The lot of the factory worker and white-collar clerk was troubling for the millions of men growing up and growing older in the Gilded Age. The Internationalists—the Communists, as they were known later—tried to paint it as a tragedy, but they didn't make much progress in America in the Gilded Age. The union movement, rocky as it was, sought more productively to remedy the new American man's disadvantage in the consolidating economy.

That still left the new American man with an even greater problem: himself.

As anyone could see, big business took a crucial sense of identity away from the individual worker, trading for it with the enticements of stability and stores full of consumer goods. However it came about, and whatever its value in the long term, big business also took power away from the individual worker. For the men of the late 1870s, weaned on the idea that power was the very prerogative of manhood, the present was hardly less confusing than the future. No longer defined by their own daily choices, they could feel just as empty as the pay envelopes that piled up to show that a life was passing by.

The unions, the political parties, and the rabble-rousers could not fill the void that so many millions of men discovered within themselves in the Gilded Age, nor could they explain just what made for a man in an age of titans.

The void had to be filled, however, and it was, almost too quickly, by the establishment of secret societies, also known as lodges. The United States, which had long been home to many different types of associations, was veritably overrun by secret societies starting quite suddenly in the 1870s. They harkened back to a previous era of self-determination and machismo, beginning in name: the Ancient Order of Foresters, the Improved Order of Redmen, and the Modern Woodmen of America, among others. Many called themselves "knights" or named themselves after virile-sounding animals like eagles, elks, or moose.

Before the Civil War, there were only a handful of secret societies. In the Gilded Age, they would proliferate. Historian Felix John Vondracek reported, "Of 568 fraternal societies whose date of organization could be ascertained, 78 were founded before 1880, 124 between 1880 and 1890, 136 between 1890 and 1895 and 230 from 1895 to 1901."[2] More important, membership grew during that span from a couple of thousand to more than five million.

One society that was probably left out of Vondracek's count was a small offshoot of the Sarsfield Guard that met locally in New Haven; it was called the Order of the Red Knights and it emphasized the brotherhood of the guard without the militarism. The Order of the Red Knights was designed to attract men who were too young to have fought in the Civil War. While the look of the group was inspired by the rising fad for fraternal groups, the particulars were invented by James Mullen, who also reigned as the Supreme Knight.[3] The Red

Knights had their own uniforms and regalia, along with formal ceremonies at the start of every meeting. The main purpose, however, was social. Although Mullen was aware of the active pursuits of the Total Abstinence societies, he didn't quite see why a person had to promise to give up drinking entirely in order to belong to a confraternity. He was, after all, a liquor dealer. His Red Knights were hardly hell-raisers, but they weren't teetotalers, either. Few lodge members were.

The Order of the Red Knights was immediately popular after its founding in 1875, and Mullen rode high on the tide it created in New Haven's social life. He was elected an alderman, serving alongside Cornelius Driscoll in the city chambers, and was appointed to the prominent position of fire commissioner.

Mullen's career was still in the ascendancy as the new decade began in 1880, but the Red Knights were starting to fade. For one thing, many of the members were getting married, a liability for any gang or purely social men's club.

William Sellwood was one of those who married. Father McGivney, his friend from the St. Joseph's Young Men's Total Abstinence and Literary Society, performed the ceremony in November 1879. In fact, Father McGivney was even closer to Sellwood's bride, Mary Ann Gaffney, another member of St. Mary's Church. All of the Gaffneys were busy and energetic people; Mary Ann and Father McGivney had many long, spirited conversations.

Aside from the attractions of marriage, there was another reason that the tepid, well-meaning Red Knights disbanded. By the early 1880s, the members had a choice of other societies, many of them with more exotic themes and even more secrecy. With most going so far as to espouse moral standards for members, the Catholic Church could not countenance them. Despite that, many Catholics joined fraternal groups, unwilling to deny either the trend of the times or the pull of their own hearts.

The situation was uncomfortable in many American cities and towns, but it came to a head in New Haven for all to see at the funeral of a Forester—that is, a member of the Ancient Order of Foresters—named John Bernhardt, an engineer at a margarine factory. Afflicted with a serious bronchial infection, he converted to Catholicism two days before he died, the sacraments being performed by Father Schaele, a local German-American priest. By the time of Bernhardt's death, however, Father Schaele was away and Father McGivney made arrangements for a funeral service at St. Mary's Church.

At the same time, Bernhardt's fellow Foresters were making plans to perform their own rites at the graveside service. Most Protestant clergymen, and some Catholic priests, allowed fraternal groups a few moments somewhere in the proceedings: at home (in the days before funeral parlors), in the church, or at the graveside.

For John Tibball, the chief ranger of the local "court" (or club) of Foresters, that was business as usual. "One of the laws of our order," he told the *New Haven Union,* "is that when the clergyman who officiates at a funeral of one of our members objects to having us perform our peculiar services at the house and grave, we shall not insist upon the point. Therefore, I asked Mrs. Bernhardt to find out whether the priest would object to our rites. She went down to Father McGivney to inquire and brought back word that the matter would be considered and we would be given a decision in the matter soon." A day later, the Foresters had McGivney's answer: "no ceremonies but those of the church would be allowed."

On the appointed morning, about forty Foresters arrived at St. Mary's in a line, decorated with their official society badges. "When the other mourners had gone in," said Tibball, "we filed up the steps two abreast. I was first in line." At the entry, the doorman at St. Mary's stopped them, saying that he "had orders to let in nobody wearing a badge." At the time, Father McGivney was standing nearby in the vestibule, greeting other mourners. It was plain to see that his authority was behind the edict. Chief Ranger Tibball turned right around.

Tibball led his Foresters to a spot under a shady tree. There, they decided not to attend the funeral at all, not without their badges. Instead, they voted to pitch in fifteen cents apiece and buy a keg of beer with which to honor the departed.

To Father McGivney, that was an unfortunate choice— not about the beer, but about placing a higher value on a bunch of badges than on the chosen church of their deceased friend. McGivney was, in his mind, simply upholding the Church's rule against admitting any civic societies not connected with the Catholic Church.[4]

"If the Foresters came in without their badges," Father McGivney told a reporter after the funeral, "they would be admitted, the same as any other persons. But they could not come in with their society badges on. The other courts of Foresters attend funerals without wearing any badges and thus avoid the difficulty."[5]

The Foresters went away grousing. "I don't understand why the priest objected," said one named John Rosinus.

"Bishop [John Joseph] Williams of Boston, I see by the papers, has advised the Catholics, if they join a secret society, to join the Foresters and has started a Catholic Foresters in his diocese. If that is the case, I think Father McGivney altogether in the wrong."

It was Chief Ranger John Tibball, however, in voicing his complaints to the *New Haven Evening Register,* who made Father McGivney's point even better than the priest had:

> We feel sorry for Mrs. Bernhardt, but don't want to say anything against the priest. We don't see the sense of his action, that's all. About half of our members are Catholics, and there are four or five courts in the city of which at least four-fifths are Catholics and Irish. We haven't anything to do with religion. I am a Catholic, that is I ought to be, and I would not object to the priest's conduct if we had anything to do with religion. But religion and politics are banished subjects from our rooms.[6]

Father McGivney did not want religion to be a banished subject from any part of the lives of Catholic men, least of all something as crucial to them as their fraternal societies.

The contretemps at John Bernhardt's funeral illustrated the dilemma facing the Church across the United States. "Americanism"—the degree to which Catholics in the United States could or would reflect the evolving values of the relatively new country—would become a consuming question in the late 1800s. Catholics struggled to reconcile their religion with factors of American life as potent as democracy, immigration, and corporate capitalism. Not coincidentally, the driving force within each of those three themes was a trait intrinsic to nearly all Americans: dissatisfaction with the status quo.

Every American was a millionaire, if only because it was always possible, however remotely, to become one. And so Americans differed radically from their nineteenth-century contemporaries in Europe and other Catholic regions. They didn't like being told to put away their dreams and return to a kind of humility that simply didn't sit well in the American character.

In the rising clash over secret societies, some priests ignored the impetuous American personality and forbade decorated members of such societies to enter churches. Other priests ignored the tenets of the Church on the subject and let anyone in, with regalia or without. Father McGivney, however, could not ignore either side. He knew firsthand that it was a much more compelling issue than even the Church realized. If secret societies were giving a lapsed Catholic like Chief Ranger Tibball his only sense of belonging, then he was much the worse for it. And so ultimately was the Church.

The members of St. Joseph's TAL, albeit not a secret society, had the best situation, in Father McGivney's view. They belonged simultaneously to the Church and to a lively group of "brothers" outside of it.

The TAL proved to be a laboratory for McGivney's ideas about his ancient religion's vitality in addressing modern life in all of its manifestations: the loneliness that ran through displaced populations; the reassessment of the role of the family in the face of technological advances that progressively decreased reliance on group living; the pressure to judge self-worth purely on a monetary basis; the availability of low-cost inebriants with the industrialization of breweries and distilleries; and a transient society's tendency to undermine the adult sense of responsibility, due to the increasingly simple and acceptable option of moving far away from inconvenient obligations. The TAL did not itself remedy all of these building pressures, but it did merge the Church more deeply into the lives of the men in the group.

In previous generations, priests were cloistered within the boundaries of their parish work, but organizations like total abstinence societies, which became common starting in the middle of the century, helped to draw them out into general society. In directing plays—and haggling with theater managers, contracting with costume companies, and paying printers—Father McGivney was part of the new trend. He was bound to the Church—but not restricted to it, as most of his predecessors, by their own choice, had been. The TAL was attached to his church, but with a great deal of independence; with this group, he felt encouraged to think that even an outside group could support the mission of a parish priest. The TAL did not interfere with Catholic teachings but emphasized them from a different perspective. In making this realization, Father McGivney could have been called a radical by his elders of the previous generation. They didn't feel that parish priests ought to place their trust in outside groups. More and more, he felt that they must.

Success on many levels naturally deepened the TAL's influence on McGivney's thinking. Nonetheless, the TAL's expansion had very definite limits. The pledge against the use of alcohol kept a great many men out and so did its focus on youthful games and activities.

Even if St. Joseph's TAL wasn't the answer to everything facing the Catholic Church in the 1880s, it could do no wrong in New Haven. In 1880, the big St. Patrick's Day show was to be *Pyke O'Callaghan, or the Patriot of '98,* a play about an intrepid servant. It was sure to draw a crowd, if only because it was a benefit for St. Mary's Church. The club optimistically rented out the 2000-seat Grand Opera House for the presentation. John Finnigan, the president, served as producer. But Billy Homer was no longer around and the play needed a director. The job fell to Father McGivney.[7]

As far as is known, *Pyke O'Callaghan* marked McGivney's debut as a theatrical director. In looking over the characters—Pyke, Sir James Blackadder, Red Rufus, the informer, Miss Honor O'Callaghan, and Lady Broughton—he made a bold decision in the name of artistic integrity: he cast females in the female parts.

Productions, large or small, of the St. Joseph's TAL had never included women before. Yale University was still clinging to the idea that men could play women's parts, but Father McGivney decided that all-male productions made no sense. He selected various women from the choirs of New Haven's Catholic churches and asked if they would take to the Grand Opera stage (the openings didn't last long). Father McGivney had another original casting idea for the British regiment that marches onstage to bully Pyke and his Irish neighbors during the course of the play. He asked James Mullen to bring in a troop of the Sarsfield Guard, with their uniforms altered to imitate British redcoats.

Eighteen hundred people were in their seats on March 17 when the curtain rose on *Pyke O'Callaghan*. Whether Father McGivney was in the appointed place of stage directors on opening night—the restroom, being sick—was not recorded. More likely, he was watching from the wings, continuing to see to details. And perhaps that is the very best place in the theater to enjoy a triumph such as *Pyke O'Callaghan* enjoyed. The cast was called back for impromptu encores and the young women in the cast were handed basket after basket of flowers.[8] Even the daily New Haven papers reviewed the sensational *Pyke* and surmised that a great deal of money for St. Mary's must have been realized.

St. Joseph's TAL went on with other fund-raising events throughout the spring of 1880. *The Connecticut Catholic* featured accounts of many of them in its columns and remarked that "too much cannot be said of the untiring efforts of the genial young priest, Father McGivney."[9]

McGivney could see how strong the group had become and in June he turned over his duties as treasurer to one of the members. Only a few months later, St. Joseph's TAL had a brush with a critic, and not a theatrical one. Someone wrote to the *Connecticut Catholic* complaining that the entertainments hosted in the group's club rooms were "of such a nature as to be injurious to the morals of the Catholic youth of the city and the cause of much scandal." The main point seemed to be that young women were joining the young men during the club's well-chaperoned literary evenings, but the idea that the St. Joseph's society was in any way "injurious to the morals of Catholic youth" was undoubtedly stinging and hurtful. The brunt of the remarks fell squarely on the man credited with shaping the group: Father Michael McGivney. He did not make any public comment himself, but the editor of the *Connecticut Catholic* replied to the criticism, "It is not the privilege of any layman to instruct the church authorities as to their duties or responsibilities."[10]

Father McGivney had not sought a public persona through his activities with the St. Joseph's TAL, but he had assumed one nonetheless. The newspapers regularly made reference to his popularity and influence. With the TAL's achievement, which he himself measured only in how many Catholic lads kept sober for another day or another year, he made himself a target. He took it in stride, but it was a lesson he would not forget. At the same time, he could not ignore the fact that Catholic men in general were facing a crisis.

In New Haven, the zeal to launch new fraternal societies continued apace in the early 1880s. Organizations came together and then often dissolved, even as they tried to catch the attention of prospective members. A group calling itself the Bachelors' Association had a hard time getting started and so it opted for the unvarnished truth, changing its name to the Jilted Club.[11] Father McGivney was more methodical in developing his own plans. With further problems between parish priests and secret societies, he clearly recognized the need for a fraternal group oriented toward Catholic men. In the autumn of 1881, he began to take action to launch his new group.

The very first thing that made McGivney's idea so extraordinary was that it came from him. An ordained representative of the Catholic Church, he was advocating the creation of an outside group. In a less liberal diocese, he would not have dared make any such suggestion. Fortunately, the atmosphere in Connecticut under Bishop McMahon was relaxed enough to allow for new ideas, if they were beneficial to Catholics. In some circles, however, the thought of a priest projecting himself into secular affairs would not have been greeted as beneficial. At best, it would be regarded as a waste of his valuable time; at worst, a tacit invitation for Catholics to depend on the group rather than the Church. But Father McGivney did not see a deep gulf between his parish work and the life of the city. Moreover, he believed that an outside group of the type he envisioned could serve Catholics as an adjunct to, not a replacement of, the Church.

Nonetheless, Father McGivney's idea was for an independent organization—not quite a secret society, but close. It was to be a civic organization, controlled by laypeople. If priests did not normally mix in civic affairs before McGivney's time, they also did not cultivate a reliance on laypeople.[12] A priest held himself at a certain remove, and tradition suggested that it was an elevated remove. In suggesting a plan by which he would work with laymen as equals, Michael McGivney was crossing into new territory. The fact that it was to be in a civic setting—and one in which the laymen would hold all of the power—made his project downright revolutionary. In smooth old Connecticut, though, there wasn't a ripple, at least not at first. Church superiors judged the plan more by its originator than its potential ramifications: Bishop McMahon and Father Lawlor saw that it was natural for McGivney to circulate with people outside of the confines of the Church, and they trusted that any project he originated must be beneficial for Catholics, or it could not have come from him.

Father McGivney envisioned a new kind of order, given

purpose by the exigencies of the times. The primary object of the proposed group, McGivney later wrote, "is to prevent people from entering *Secret Societies*, by offering the same, if not better, advantages to our members. Secondly, to unite the men of our Faith throughout the Diocese of Hartford, that we may thereby gain strength *to aid* each other in time of sickness; to *provide* for decent burial, and to render pecuniary assistance to the families of deceased members."[13]

To gauge the potential interest in such a club, he called a preliminary meeting, for Sunday afternoon, October 2, 1881. It was to be held in the basement hall of St. Mary's Church, although men from all parishes were invited. Not many specifics were disclosed in advance. For the time being, the only real basis for the organization was that Father McGivney was associated with it.

9

MCGIVNEY'S SOLUTION

William Geary and Cornelius Driscoll were among those who intended to go to the meeting at St. Mary's in early October 1881. In an unpublished memoir that they later completed together, they described Father McGivney at the time. "He was a young priest, a great favorite with the people," they wrote, continuing that McGivney was particularly popular "with the energetic, pushing, go-ahead young men. He was about 27 years of age [sic] and was of slight build, weighing about one hundred and fifty pounds. He possessed a captivating smile, and an earnestness of manner that he imparted to all whose interest and influence he sought."[1]

In large measure because of that McGivney charisma, eighty men showed up at the meeting. By the time it ended, a committee of twelve had been appointed to lay the groundwork for a new organization composed of Catholic men: a group that was benevolent, fraternal, and soundly religious. In a later meeting at Cornelius Driscoll's law office, James T. Mullen was elected chairman and Father McGivney secretary. There it might have stayed—a committee of well-meaning, very busy men—if not for McGivney. "It was always in a vein of seriousness and optimism of the success of the project that he counseled with his associates," Driscoll and Geary recalled, "and he would not be put off with promises they would look into the matter."

For Michael McGivney, even such an air of insistence was something new. His own previous experience had tended toward scholarly solitude. Yet in his work with the TAL, he discovered that he possessed considerable leadership ability. Part of it stemmed from his stature as a parish priest. When people look up to a person, it is rather easy for him to stand tall. The greater part of McGivney's leadership sense, however, was innate. He knew when to be stern and when to ease off, when to press his own views and when to stand aside. He had the right instincts, at least in giving direction to the laborers and music-shop assistants of the TAL. Trying to spark the somewhat older crowd of lawyers and businessmen sitting in Driscoll's office was another story. They were a more aggressive lot. While they heartily acknowledged to one another or anyone else around town that Father McGivney was a great leader, they didn't act on any of his suggestions.

With everyone else procrastinating, it was Michael McGivney who took action that fall. Having generally avoided fraternal groups for years, he was suddenly called upon to become an expert on them. If, after all, someone had already formed a Catholic organization similar to the one he envisioned, then there would be no need to start from scratch. With that in mind, he visited Boston in November to meet with members of the Order of Catholic Foresters, the outfit sanctioned by Bishop Williams. The Catholic Foresters seemed to be well organized and McGivney returned with the notion of simply establishing a "court" in New Haven. At any rate, it was a matter for further investigation over the coming months.

The men who attended the preliminary meeting at St. Mary's were aware that the new order would be a benevolent organization: that is, it would provide some sort of payout in case of sickness or death. That meant that Father McGivney also had to delve into the subject of insurance and read all of the fine print, of which there was always plenty. Fortunately, he was in the right state in which to immerse himself in that subject. Although personal insurance had been established first in Philadelphia (by Benjamin Franklin), Connecticut had taken a lead in sales and innovation in the mid-nineteenth century. Companies such as Connecticut General, Aetna, Connecticut Mutual, and Travelers, all based in Hartford, covered the country with policies.[2]

For all of the advances, however, members of the working class and middle class—"practical men," in the expression of the day—generally steered clear of the insurance industry. In the first place, repeated financial scandals frightened prospective customers. Secondly, commercial life insurance policies were typically designed for people with substantial assets.[3] Most workingmen, white collar or blue, looked to benevolent societies to share the risk of being alive.

Father Michael
Joseph McGivney.
*(Photo archives, Knights
of Columbus Supreme
Council)*

A priest gives his blessing to Irish villagers forced out of their homes by
famine or eviction.
(Illustrated London News, *May 10, 1851*)

The graduating class at East Main Street School, Waterbury, 1865. Michael McGivney is seated at far left.
(Salvatore J. Santopietro Collection, Photo archives, Knights of Columbus Supreme Council)

Winter scene at Our Lady of Angels Seminary, Niagara University, overlooking Niagara Falls.
(Niagara University)

Baseball box score printed in the *Niagara Indexensis* for June 1, 1872, listing McGivney as batting cleanup and playing left field for the Charter Oaks. *(Niagara University)*

St. Mary's Church, New Haven, as it appeared during Father McGivney's tenure as assistant pastor there. *(Photo archives, Knights of Columbus Supreme Council)*

BASE BALL.

May 20th, 1872.

Editor *Index Niagarensis*—

DEAR SIR:

Appended, please find the score of a match game of base ball played between the "Mohawks" and "Charter Oaks," both of the Seminary.—Game called on the fifth inning:

MOHAWKS.

	R.	O.
Grace, c.	1.	2.
Kearns, p.	2.	1.
Russell, 1. b.	1.	2.
Hall, 2 b	1.	1.
Barrett, 3 b	0.	2.
O'Connor, s. s.	0.	3.
Delaney, l. f.	0.	1.
Kernan, c. f.	0.	2.
Lee, r. f.	1.	1.
Total,	6.	15.

CHARTER OAKS.

	R.	O.
Hanlon, 1. b.	2.	3.
Don Levy, r. f.	3.	1.
Ring, s. s.	3.	2.
McGivney, l. f.	3.	2.
Pope, c.	3.	1.
Growney, c. f.	3.	1.
Welch, 3. b.	1.	2.
Splain, p.	2.	2.
O'Grady, 2. b.	3.	1.
Total,	23.	15.

Umpire,   T. E. Donnelly.

Scorers,   Messrs. Byrnes & Kelly.

The prompt and correct judgments of the honorable umpire elicited applause from the members of both clubs, and their thanks are tendered to him for the gentlemanly manner in which he acquitted himself of that onerous duty.

The Charter Oak B. B. C., which has begun its career with such marked success, is of recent origin; and the manner in which the members conducted themselves in their *début* among the ball tossers of the Seminary, must inspire them with just hopes of future success. The officers chosen to conduct the affairs of the club are as follows:

President,	Jno. J. Splain.
Vice "	M. J. McGivney.
Secretary,	C. M. Pope.
Treasurer,	Jas. Sullivan.
Captain,	R. O'Grady.

Chas. M. Pope,

Sec. Charter Oak B. B. C.

The Green, the hub of New Haven life, on a snowy day, circa 1880.
(Connecticut Historical Society, Hartford)

Downes stationery store, New Haven.
(Courtesy of Paul Keroac

David Hillhouse Buel, Yale
University class of 1883.
(George W. Johnston et al, Yale 1883:
The Book of the Class Compiled
after its Quartercentenary
Reunion, *New Haven, CT: Tuttle,*
Morehouse & Taylor, 1910)

Lawrence McMahon,
bishop of Hartford from
1879 to 1894.
(Hartford Diocese)

Members of the Order of Knights

NAME.	Age.	Council.	No.	Location.	Nativity.	Occupation.	Init.
McGivney M. J. Rev. J.	3	Dead aug 14 90 San Salvador 1	1	New Haven	Waterbury	Clergyman	Feb. 2
Mullen Jas. T.	39	Dead 1/6 1891		"	New Haven	Merchant	"
Colwell Daniel	36			"	Massachusetts		"
Kerrigan John T.	28			"	New Haven	Postal Clerk	"
Geary Wm. M.	31	"	"	"	"	Clerk	"
McMahon Jas. T.	29	"	"	"	"	Carriage Mkr	"
Driscoll Cornelius T.	35	"	"	"	Ireland	Lawyer	"
Curran Michael	37	Died May 7/95	"	"	"	Undertaker	"
O'Connor Matthew C.	33	"	"	"	"	Physician	"

Ledger of Knights of Columbus San Salvador Council #1, showing
that Father McGivney was the very first member.
(Archives, Knights of Columbus Supreme Council)

The founders of the Knights of Columbus, Father McGivney at the center. Clockwise from the top: William M. Geary, John T. Kerrigan, Daniel Colwell, James McMahon, Cornelius T. Driscoll, Matthew C. O'Connor, M.D., Michael Tracey, James T. Mullen, William Sellwood.
(Columbiad, archives, Knights of Columbus Supreme Council)

Father McGivney, circa 1882. The setting may be the St. Mary's rectory or a studio decorated to look like it. *(Photo archives, Knights of Columbus Supreme Council)*

James "Chip" Smith, convicted of murdering a policeman and sentenced to hang in New Haven. (New Haven Evening Register, *September 19, 1882)*

Tiffany & Co. flask for sacramental wine, engraved "Rev. Father M.J. McGiveney [sic] from A.M." Gift is attributed to Annie McGivney, the priest's sister.
(Salvatore J. Santopietro Collection)

St. Thomas Church in Thomaston, Connecticut. This picture, taken September 1, 1884, shows people arriving for the funeral of Rev. Eugene Gaffney. Father McGivney, who was present at the funeral, later succeeded Father Gaffney as pastor of St. Thomas Church.
(Photo archives, Knights of Columbus Supreme Council)

Father McGivney went at the challenge of organizing just such a society for Catholic men with an entrepreneurial zeal. No chore was too much trouble, no reading too dull—and no acquaintance immune from his enthusiasm for the idea. Fortunately, his own pastor, Father Lawlor, was in favor of it. But in McGivney's mind, the New Haven club would not be an end unto itself. Instead, he thought of it as a model for groups throughout the Hartford Diocese. That sort of ambition is right and natural in a twenty-nine-year-old, but it also encompassed dozens of other priests in his dream, and that brought in a host of human qualities.

In early November, Father McGivney wrote to a long list of Connecticut priests, informing them that a committee in New Haven was addressing the need for a Catholic fraternal club. It was around that time that Father McGivney learned that Father Thomas Walsh of Meriden, for one, was taking a dim view of the movement. At fifty-seven, Father Walsh was the oldest priest in the diocese. He was also the pastor of Meriden's biggest parish, St. Rose's. Most of all, though, he served as vicar-general of the Hartford Diocese, an administrative position that made him second in rank to Bishop McMahon. Father Walsh, who had once been lenient about letting members of secret societies wear their regalia in his church, had recently taken a harsh stand against men's societies of all kinds, Catholic or not. Even as Father McGivney trumpeted his idea around most of his fellow priests, he tiptoed around Father Walsh.

The picture of Father McGivney in November 1881 was of a man without time to rest. With papers, books, and letters under his arm, he called on his fellow committeemen at their homes or in their offices to complete the research phase of the creation of the club, detail by detail. Returning home, he would set his papers down at the rectory and just have time to attend to his spiritual duties, performing nine marriages and six baptisms during the month. Possibly in deference to the constraints on his time, the parish managed to stay healthy and there were no funerals.

December was not as kind. Edward Downes Sr. died, leaving a gap in the whole Irish-American community. "Mr. Downes was one of the most prominent and most popular of New Haven's business men," eulogized the *Connecticut Catholic*, "and withal a sincere and zealous Catholic."[4] Father McGivney, close to every member of the family, knew a bit more than that. Downes, the city's leading stationer, was prominent and popular, but he was also practically broke. Father McGivney officiated at the funeral Mass and then consoled the family. He didn't stop there.

Josephine Downes, the former organist at St. Mary's, was a novice at Mount St. Joseph's Convent in Hartford. Edward Jr. was studying for the priesthood at Father McGivney's alma mater, St. Mary's in Baltimore. The other children were at home with Mrs. Downes, and some of them went to bed on the night of the funeral wondering whether they would be allowed to remain there.

In the late nineteenth century, a widow in Catherine Downes's position could expect to join the ranks of the impoverished. Few married women—only 5 percent—held jobs in the paid workforce. Those who did received on average 46 percent of a man's wages.[5] New Haven had enough of a heart, and enough of a tax base, to provide temporary assistance for the poor, but no government agency in the United States in those days provided continuing support.

In the scenario typical in the 1800s, Mrs. Downes would have to find work and those children who couldn't join her in earning money would go to the orphanage. Father McGivney helped her in a concerted effort to make sure that it wouldn't come to that. The first step, unfortunately, was Edward Jr.'s withdrawal from the seminary.

The priesthood was a calling that usually involved support, if not sacrifice, from the whole family. Edward's family was in no position to offer either one. Quite the opposite: he had to come home and run the store, with his sister Mary. Josephine stayed at the convent, in part because she was within a year of taking her vows as a nun. Anyway, her health was uncertain: she had chronic breathing problems and no one could be sure how she would fare outside of the quiet atmosphere of the convent.

Mrs. Downes's most pressing problem was proving to the court that her teenage son Alfred would be cared for and that he would not become a public charge. The judge would require a substantial bond, signed by two different guarantors, and for that, the family turned to Father McGivney. His sympathies lay entirely with the family, and with Alfred's dream of attending college. On a practical basis, any priest connected to a church with a $165,000 debt knew exactly which parishioners had money. He might be able to find someone to guarantee the bond.

Through it all, McGivney didn't miss a step in collecting information for the new men's organization. During a visit to New Haven, Bishop McMahon spared time to listen to Father

McGivney and a small delegation of laymen outline their plans. Sister Delores Liptak, in her rich history of the Hartford Diocese, wrote that "they gained Bishop McMahon's implicit permission to form a fraternal benefit society that would transcend parish boundaries in its efforts to assist fellow Catholics."[6]

In mid-January 1882, Father McGivney visited Brooklyn, where the Catholic Benevolent League (CBL) had been started the previous September. It offered life insurance benefits, limited sickness disbursements, and "programs for social and intellectual improvement."[7]

All in all, the CBL was admirable, but a little dry as the model for a club that was supposed to compete with the fascination of the secret societies. Anyway, Father McGivney was ill impressed with the sick benefits it offered. For good measure, he visited Boston once more, to meet with the Catholic Foresters.

On returning home, having caught a bad cold, Father McGivney decided that he was quite satisfied with the Catholic Foresters and he duly wrote to the secretary, Michael Edmonds, proposing that the New Haven contingent form themselves into a court. To his utter astonishment, the suggestion was rejected.

Edmonds made some weak reference to the Catholic Foresters' state charter, which enabled it to operate only within Massachusetts (that could have been changed, quite easily).[8] In truth, the men in charge just weren't ready to oversee far-flung Foresters.

The Catholic Benevolent League, on the other hand, was all set to expand into Connecticut, according to a report published in the *Connecticut Catholic*. The committee of New Haven men met again on February 2. Interest was still keen and there were only two absentees. Father McGivney described his visits to Brooklyn and Boston, leaving out the part about catching a cold in Boston, and then, according to the minutes of that meeting, he "advised against affiliating with the CBL and further reported that the Mass. Catholic Order of Foresters could not accept us as insurance risks. At the close of the report, a motion was made and unanimously carried that 'we organize a purely original organization.' "[9]

Father McGivney had arrived prepared for that eventuality. The first order of business was selecting a name for the new outfit. There were those at the meeting who liked the sound of "Connecticut Order of Catholic Foresters." It would save time in future conversations about the new outfit, since most people knew of the Foresters, Catholic or otherwise. To Father McGivney, that was the problem with that name: it was burdened with its own connotations. A "purely original organization" should have its own identity from the start. But he waited to hear what the others might think. They showed that they certainly had their priorities.

According to Geary and Driscoll, "the titles of the Officers in the Foresters, as the Committee gathered them from different sources, did not appeal to them." They didn't want to be known as Ranger Bill and Ranger Cornelius.

Another point raised against borrowing the name "Catholic Foresters" was of greater interest to Father McGivney. It represented the departure of the new group from all that had gone before. "Although the association was to be composed of Catholic men only," Geary and Driscoll explained, recalling the discussion at the February 2 meeting, the committee members "thought the name or prefix 'Catholic' would impress many persons as a Church society or sodality, and the organization would not in the lapse of time be permanent." That killed the name for Father McGivney. In his view, the club had to be launched, even from the nucleus of twelve committeemen, without limits on its growth.

McGivney waited for the discussion to run its course. And then, in the lull of ideas that followed the consensus against Connecticut Order of Catholic Foresters, he suggested "Sons of Columbus."

Christopher Columbus being Italian, it was a remarkable proposal to make to a committee composed entirely of Irish-Americans. Aside from Reverend McGivney, the roll call that day consisted of Messrs. Carroll, Colwell, Driscoll, Geary, Healy, Kerrigan, McMahon, Mullen, and O'Connor. Yet they realized at once the brilliance of the idea. Even in the anti-Catholic climate of the late nineteenth century, Columbus figured as a national hero.

A few years before, the *Connecticut Catholic* had run a front-page editorial on the importance of the explorer:

> Although it may be, and we believe is true that the Northmen discovered and made settlements in Greenland and new England in the ninth and tenth centuries, yet this fact does not dim by one iota the true fame and merit of Columbus. As American Catholics, we do not know of anyone who more deserves our grateful remembrance than the great and noble man—the pious, zealous, and the faithful

Catholic—the enterprising navigator, and the large-hearted sailor, Christopher Columbus—"The Christ Bearing Dove" as his name signifies.[10]

In the climate of the 1880s, the name Columbus affirmed that the New Haven organization would be loyal to the United States; that was a constant, if unfounded, point of suspicion where Catholics were concerned. At the same time, it would encourage Catholics of all nationalities to join: Connecticut was already home to many French-Canadian and German Catholics, and Italians were arriving in ever increasing numbers. Assimilating them was Bishop McMahon's most pressing challenge. Even as he fought to dispel the idea that Connecticut Catholicism was Irish Catholicism, the non-Gaelic reference in the name was certain to appeal to him as an aid to his effort.

There was only one problem with McGivney's suggested name: "Sons." Every man on the committee, and every man everywhere, was already a son. But fraternalism was also about aspiration, if not outright fantasy. James Mullen immediately pointed out that "Knights" would be a better noun to use.[11] There was nothing especially original about the use of "knights"; the world was already full of them, including the Knights of Pythias, Knights of St. Patrick, Knights of the Maccabees, Knights Templar, and Knights of Honor. After all, what male wouldn't want to be a knight, in or out of shining armor—it was the universal ideal of manhood. But it wasn't just a word that fired up James Mullen.

"Mr. Mullen," recalled Daniel Colwell, who was there, "amended it [McGivney's suggested name] by making it

'Knights of Columbus,' stating with much force that if we intended to have a society, we must have one of ritualistic form, that it was only such that would hold the men together."[12]

According to the minutes of the meeting, "it was moved, seconded and carried that the society be known as the 'Connecticut Knights of Columbus.'"

That brought the committee directly to the next order of business: "On motion it was voted that we make it a ritualistic society."[13]

Michael McGivney was interested least of all in the ritual aspect of the society—the hierarchy of degrees, the design of regalia, the choreography of ceremonies—but it was a necessary component of a fraternal group, according to the others. James Mullen volunteered to work out the details of the degrees, along with the ceremonies and passwords to be used. Without compelling ceremonies, the members would not feel that it was a special privilege to be a Knight of Columbus, and so Father McGivney cooperated with the formation of the secret aspects of the new society. Later, once Mullen and the others had worked out such details, from the leader's title of "Supreme Knight" down through the symbolism of the rites, Father McGivney expressed his opinion that "the titles etc. it is true are a little high-strung."[14] However, he was adamant on the point that the Knights operate entirely in line with the Church, although officially separate from it. "Father McGivney advised that all the ritual and secret work be laid before the Bishop of the Diocese, Bishop Lawrence S. McMahon," Geary and Driscoll wrote.[15]

Losing no time, the fledgling Knights called a general meeting for Monday, February 6, at St. Mary's. In starting out that day, Father McGivney had to push through more than a foot of fresh snow left by the winter skies—and by the people who were supposed to shovel the walks. The meeting took up some of his thoughts, but not all of them. It wasn't even the most important event of his day. There was a baptism for a baby named Carol Cullen, and then there was the hearing to determine the guardianship status of Alfred Downes. Father McGivney had arranged that he would stand as principal for the young man, by means of a probate bond. Because of his intervention, the Downeses remained together as a family. He had become familiar with such processes in his research on behalf of the new benevolent society. McGivney was quite a different man than he had been upon graduating from seminary. He knew how to work the law, he understood business principles, and he had begun to learn the nuances of publicity. In his view, being a priest did not keep him from playing a part in the wider world; to the contrary, in dire cases such as the one before him in probate court, it compelled him to do so.

McGivney returned to the rectory after the hearing, with barely a moment to spare for dinner before men began to stream along Hillhouse Avenue, headed for St. Mary's. To his delight, seventy-five men gave up their warm easy chairs to brave the frigid temperatures and attend the meeting.

The newspapers also started to take interest in the new group, but Father McGivney learned from the very start what a mixed blessing that can be. At least, the *Morning Journal* had it right: "The first meeting of those interested in the Catholic organization known as the Knights of Columbus was held in St. Mary's church Monday evening."[16]

"A preliminary meeting of the Catholic order of Foresters

was held Monday night," reported the *Evening Register,* erro-
neously.[17] The paper should have known better; the night editor was John J. Splain, Father McGivney's baseball teammate
from Our Lady of Angels Seminary. One of Splain's reporters
was young Stephen Maher, who had attended St. Charles's
College in Maryland, believing himself headed for the priesthood. After graduating, however, he changed his mind and
went to work for the *Evening Register.* Maher attended the
meeting at St. Mary's and even decided to join the Knights of
Columbus. Despite his enthusiasm, he couldn't remember the
right name when he filed his story.

At the beginning of March, an early spring took hold of New
Haven. Female students from the Yale Art School were spotted
with their easels all over town: sketching an old fish market, an
even older rag shop, and then the sunset on the harbor. The first
baseball practice also sprang up, another sign of the season.[18]

The turn in the weather only made Father McGivney more
intent, as though time were wasting. At the March 1 meeting,
he "urged that all committees having work in hand should be-
stir themselves that everything might be in readiness."[19]

As McGivney reported at the meeting, he had already
written a circular that had been sent to parishes in the diocese.
He would continue to send out such circulars on a monthly
basis. His own words not only describe the group but indicate
that his priority lay with the practicalities:

> The aid to which the family of a deceased mem-
> ber shall be entitled is regulated by the grade to which

such member belongs in the Endowment fund. This fund consists of three grades of payments: viz.: five hundred dollars for the first grade; one thousand for the second grade, and fifteen hundred dollars for the third grade; the assessments when a death occurs being fifty cents for those belonging to first grade, one dollar for those in second grade and one dollar and fifty cents for those insuring in the third grade.

Besides this Fund there is a Sick Benefit Deposit, from which a member in good standing at the time of his sickness may draw a sum amounting to not more than five dollars per week for thirteen weeks, the amount to be given thereafter, if sickness continues, to be regulated by the Council to which the member belongs.

The ages of admission are from eighteen to fifty years.

The necessity for such an organization will readily manifest itself by a glance at the rolls of the various secret societies in this State. The number of men of our Faith already belonging to and daily joining these societies is very great, and nothing but the absence of an organization such as we have effected, has led to this lamentable fact.[20]

In the way that Father McGivney had organized the insurance, nearly anyone could afford coverage. His sick benefit of five dollars per week was equivalent to about 63 percent of the average weekly wages for a man in his thirties or forties. According to the same average, the top-level death payout, $1500, was equal to about four years' earnings. At that, it was about $200 more than an average price for a home in the 1880s.[21] A system of support such as that might have made all the difference in the world to Catherine Downes and countless other widows like her.

On St. Patrick's Day, Father McGivney once again served as the director of the St. Joseph's TAL show, or extravaganza. In its burgeoning form, the production included a play, with vaudeville-style acts before and after. According to some reports, Father McGivney even had a speaking part in the play, but he certainly presided over a banquet afterward for the members of St. Joseph's TAL and their dates. Also invited, perhaps not too coincidentally, were the members of a similar TAL group from the town of Meriden. Naturally, the dinner conversation turned to the new Knights of Columbus, and the Meriden men went home fully versed in the plans for the new group.

On March 29, the assembly of the state of Connecticut formally recognized the Knights of Columbus with a charter. Three days later, the first members of the Knights of Columbus were initiated in a ceremony at St. Mary's Church. The names were familiar as members of Father McGivney's circle—Cornelius Driscoll, James T. Mullen, William Sellwood, Edward Downes Jr., John Finnegan, and so forth. With the Knights of Columbus established, McGivney's circle could keep expanding, and it never had to stop.

10

A BLEAK NIGHT IN ANSONIA

For all of Michael McGivney's activities and his acknowledged popularity, he was not even close to being New Haven's biggest celebrity in the spring of 1882. Neither he nor anyone else received so much as one-tenth of the attention paid to James "Chip" Smith.

At Christmastime two years before, Smith was an unemployed twenty-one-year-old, living with his parents and younger sister in the town of Ansonia, about five miles west of New Haven. He was known to Daniel J. Hayes, the chief of police, as a ruffian, but generally a harmless one. That Christmas was particularly hard on Hayes, who had a gravely ill four-year-old child at home. Nonetheless, he was out making his usual rounds on December 28. Chip Smith was drunk that night, carousing with Hayes's brother in fact, and causing trouble by shooting off a pistol near a saloon. When Smith's father heard that his son had gotten hold of a gun somewhere, he asked Dan Hayes to locate him and take him into custody. Chief Hayes found Smith alone, and reeling, outside of a theater on Main Street in Ansonia. Hayes tried to handcuff him, but Smith wriggled away.

Just as their tussle turned into an all-out wrestling match, Smith said that he would surrender quietly if Hayes would just let go. Hayes released his grasp, pulling out his revolver as he did. In the next instant, Smith had a gun in his hand, too. One of the pistols went off.

"I'm shot," Hayes groaned, but he still clung to Smith to keep him from escaping. Even though a crowd gathered, no one came to Hayes's aid. Finally, the police chief called out to a passerby that he knew, and practically demanded help. As the two of them tried to subdue the drunken Smith, he was still pulling the trigger on his gun. It clicked past empty chambers. As soon as Smith was in custody, Hayes was taken to a nearby house and the severity of his wound was discovered. Within a few hours, he died. His wife went into a kind of shock on hearing the news. Then, the next morning, their child died, too.

Smith didn't seem to care about any of it. At his arraignment the next day, he was still very much the street tough. The first witness, questioned by the judge, related the story of the fight. When the judge then asked Smith if he was represented by counsel, he replied, "No, I don't want no counsel." The judge asked him if he wanted to question the witness himself. "No, I don't want to ask him anything," Smith said. "He is telling a pack of damned lies."

"I am not," the witness said.

"Yes, you are," Smith sneered. "You were not there, when I was arrested."[1]

At the actual trial in New Haven the following April, Smith finally had a good lawyer, who unfortunately had not had much time to prepare. Many people commented on the fact that Smith's expression barely changed at all during the course of the trial. "Perhaps he don't know enough to appreciate the real danger his life is in," a court clerk suggested. When the verdict was read, he found out. Chip Smith was convicted of murder in the first degree, for which the sentence was execution.[2]

All New Haven had come to know Smith during the famous trial. According to his own lawyer, he was a man of diminished capacity, either simple in intellect or slightly "demented." Whatever Smith's state, Father Michael McGivney was already aware of it.

McGivney was a regular visitor to New Haven's jail, offering spiritual support to the prisoners. In Chip Smith, he found a person in terrible need. They visited together often in Smith's cell—a double cell, actually, arranged by a kindly jailer. The atmosphere in the New Haven County Jail was relaxed, compared with others around the country, and Smith was not reviled there, despite the heinous accusation against him. Friends in Ansonia sent cheerful gifts, including a canary for company. It sat in a cage near the door, oblivious of the emotions all around, singing merrily. Smith had photographs of his guards and some of their children tacked to his wall. He also had several pictures of himself. He would gaze at one or another of them for a long time, and then pace the cell.

For more than a year, Father McGivney counseled Smith, and brought him closer and closer to the church into which he had been born, but which he had forsaken early in life. During that time, Smith's fate was uncertain, as legal motions seeking to amend his conviction were duly filed before the appellate courts.

The case was an interesting one. Smith insisted that it was Hayes's own gun that had discharged, delivering the mortal wound. Most prisoners, it is true, have some such story to underscore their blameless innocence; however, on another point, Smith did seem to have some hope. Part of the definition of first-degree murder in Connecticut was that the crime had to have been premeditated. Smith certainly didn't seem to have planned the shooting in advance. He had, after all, been accosted by Hayes, not the other way around. On that basis, Smith's lawyer argued that the conviction should be reduced to second-degree murder and the sentence changed to life in prison. When the appeal seemed to be on its way to success, Smith admitted to a reporter that he dreaded the thought of hanging.[3]

Still, a policeman had been shot. For that reason, judges simply could not muster much sympathy for Chip Smith. His appeal was denied. In March 1882, his supporters placed a resolution commuting the sentence before the state legislature. On the fifteenth, the legislature addressed the resolution. That day, Father McGivney was busy with his own happy affairs—rehearsing the St. Joseph's variety show and seeing to late details on the formation of the Knights of Columbus. The next morning, the papers carried the news from Hartford that the

House had rejected a commutation for Smith by "an over-whelming vote."[4]

The execution was scheduled for May 5 but was delayed by further motions filed by Smith's lawyer. Life had long since lost its connection to reality for Smith, as hope for legal dispensation came and went, came again and was snatched away. Only one source of hope was constant. "Father McGivney visits me very often," Smith told a reporter from the *New Haven Union* during the summer, "and I think a great deal of him."[5]

Few people knew yet about Father McGivney's work with Smith, but many were coming to know of his affiliation with the Knights of Columbus. In the early days, Driscoll and Geary recalled, McGivney warned "we will meet with obstacles and even rebuffs, but with God's help, we would not fail."[6]

McGivney was right: there were obstacles in the early going; the only surprise was where they came from. Not the anti-Catholics in the community, not the reactionary members of the Church, either. The order's most vitriolic criticism came from within, as the founding officers started a long and tiresome round of infighting. One of the men in the middle of it was William Geary himself. And so perhaps it is fitting that he was the first one to suffer the consequences of the fruitless feuding.

In late April, Geary was climbing into his carriage when he slipped somehow and fell hard on the ground. His leg was broken just above the ankle. As the doctor set it, he predicted that Geary would be bedridden for eight weeks.[7] With the Knights of Columbus still in formation, Geary couldn't expect any sick benefits; there were not yet enough members to allow for claims. Until the leaders stopped bickering, the number wasn't likely to rise very quickly. Geary, however, was out of the fray for the time being.

Father McGivney's role was to keep the founders from losing sight of the horizon, with all of their picayune disputes over regalia and colors—and which one among them wasn't pulling his weight. If McGivney had been asked in a candid moment, he would have said that none of them were. In late April, he was distracted for the better by the annual fair to benefit St. Mary's Church. It wasn't the only entertainment to be had in New Haven, however. The fair started the same week as an exhibition of the midget stars General and Mrs. Tom Thumb, as well as a phenomenally popular production of a musical called *Penikeese,* which had been written by David Hillhouse Buel, Father McGivney's friend at Yale. The full title was *Penikeese; or Cuisine and Cupid.*[8] Patterned after the operettas of Gilbert and Sullivan and plump with local jokes, it had outgrown its student production and was being staged professionally in New Haven. Buel was much admired, a star for greater New Haven, but the attention he was receiving didn't interfere with his abiding respect for his old friend. He still attended St. Mary's Church to hear McGivney say Mass and deliver his sermons.

Despite having so much competition for the bon vivants of New Haven, St. Mary's fair did excellent business. For Michael McGivney, it was also something of a reunion, as he hosted his old friend, Father Carmody, on a turn through the fair.[9] Later, another friend, Reverend Foley of Brooklyn, paid a visit; he had been at Our Lady of Angels with McGivney.

Another classmate from the Niagara days also came into town during the early weeks of the fair: James Splain, Father McGivney's first and best friend at the school, was home for a stay with his parents in New Haven. Splain's father, also named James, was a common laborer, yet he and his wife had seen nearly all of their children graduate from college. John Splain was still the night editor of the *Evening Register*. Like John, James (the younger) had veered away from the priesthood after college, deciding instead on medicine and taking a degree at New York University. His inborn generosity and fund of bright humor—along with considerable skill, no doubt—enabled him to build a successful practice in New Haven in the late 1870s, when Father McGivney was just starting at St. Mary's. Dr. Splain, however, had a sister in San Francisco, and he heard enough about the opportunity there to move out in 1880. In a short time, he built another burgeoning practice. It didn't last.

Splain had to give it all up and return to his parents' house in New Haven when he contracted tuberculosis. He may not have been strong enough to visit the St. Mary's fair, but he certainly renewed his friendship with Father McGivney as soon as he was back in town.

On Monday, May 22, the fair finally ended, with a $440 profit to set against the debt at St. Mary's. On Saturday, the Splain boys' father was on a crew working at a house that was being renovated. Told to clear a pile of dirt out of a cellar, he was standing over it, about to get to work, when the wall

above him suddenly caved in and crushed him. Father Mc-
Givney was summoned immediately and he rushed to the
scene, arriving just in time to administer the last rites.

A year that had started with so much vibrance in its outlook was turning into a notably dank spring. Father Lawlor
wasn't well,[10] and many of his duties were left to Father Mc-
Givney. McGivney's position was reminiscent of his first summer at St. Mary's, when Father Murphy, worn down by
worries over the church debt, was too sick to fulfill his obligations. Father Lawlor was suffering from the same grinding
stress.

On top of that, the Knights of Columbus membership
was stalled at twenty-seven—well short of the goal and certainly not enough to promise any benefits. In early June,
Michael McGivney wrote to Michael Edmonds, the secretary
of the Order of Catholic Foresters, who had expressed a
friendly interest in the Connecticut group. As was, it seems,
usual for McGivney, he started out by apologizing for his delay in responding. "The Order I was endeavoring to establish
fell back almost lifeless but not dead," he admitted, "and . . . I
did not want to write without having something to tell you
about our success." McGivney blamed the lack of action on
the cold that he had caught in Boston the previous January.
That might have stalled the organizational efforts for days, but
not for months. As it was, Father McGivney was forced to recognize that his leadership skills were having little effect in mo-
tivating the men at the core of the Knights of Columbus. At
times, even for the best generals, there is nothing to do but wait
for something to happen, something that offers a new chance to
act—and, meanwhile, to keep the group from disintegrating.

McGivney was dismayed, frustrated, and understandably perplexed, but he wasn't yet pessimistic. "Our beginning is extremely slow," Father McGivney reflected in his letter to
Edmonds, "but I think that when our By-laws are distributed
we will advance more rapidly."[11] With just a bit of desperation, Father McGivney asked Stephen Maher to put a squib in
the *Evening Register* in mid-June: "The object of this association," it concluded, after listing the officers, "is to promote the
principles of unity and charity, so that the members may gain
strength to bestow charity on each other. . . . Further information will be furnished by Rev. M.J. McGivney to all who
apply."[12]

Father McGivney, who had not had a vacation since arriving at St. Mary's Church four years before, renewed himself
through daily prayer and the retreats that were, sagaciously
enough, mandatory for parish priests. Without these two opportunities for renewal, a priest would be worn out in practically no time. Aside from these forms of respite, however,
Father McGivney wasn't likely to have any time off in the
summer of 1882. To counter the many dark and draining calls
he had to make on the troubled, he did at least have various
picnics to attend. Aside from the fact that he organized two of
them, he could relax at the grassy outings and see the ball
games or watch the picnickers dance away the afternoon. In
early August, however, both he and Father Lawlor preached
strong sermons against the vogue for unchaperoned dances,
many of which occurred at night. Father McGivney, who
liked nothing more than the idea of young people having fun,
wasn't moved by any pressure to be modern on the subject of
such rendezvous. "Too many of our young Catholic men get

up these afternoon and evening picnics and much harm results from them," he said, according to a summary of his remarks. "If they want a day of enjoyment, why not attend the church picnics which will give them good innocent pleasure and where their money will be put to some good and faithful use."[13]

Coloring the whole summer for Father McGivney and the rest of New Haven was the specter of Chip Smith's imminent execution, which had been conclusively scheduled for Friday, September 1. Father McGivney had long since become a daily visitor, as had nuns from the convent of the Sisters of Mercy.

During the last week of August, the governor of Connecticut made it clear that he was not inclined to offer Smith a reprieve. It was really going to happen.

Inside the jail, Chip Smith, humanely tolerated at first, had become of all things a favorite. Though it is odd to say it, he was actually beloved by the guards. Without liquor, Smith was a heartbreakingly sweet-natured fellow. Unfortunately, as friends of the family confirmed, his stay in jail was the first time in his whole life that he had been without liquor, either on his breath or his father's. The transformation went even deeper than Smith's reclaimed self-control, however. A reporter from the *Evening Register* visited him during his last week:

> At the office of the county jail, there is observable among the attendants an unusual air of solemnity. The man least affected by the execution to occur Friday morning is Smith himself. He has undergone a change in the past few weeks which would make him

almost unrecognizable to those who knew him as a tough specimen among the rougher mechanics in Ansonia or have seen him, dull, expressionless and apparently devoid of ordinary intelligence in the court room. The ministrations of Father McGivney and the Sisters of Mercy have given him the full consolation conveyed by strong and sincere religious faith. He has lately had an unwonted animation of countenance and cheerfulness of spirits which can be accounted for on no other ground.[14]

Although Father McGivney's own faith was strong, the long path on which he led Chip Smith was exhausting for him. He was expected to stay with Smith throughout the ordeal on September 1. He sometimes doubted that he would be able to hold up. Even the man best prepared for a repellent duty can be disturbed by it.

On the Sunday before the execution, Father McGivney celebrated a High Mass for Chip Smith at the jail. His sermon, such as it was—a eulogy in advance—was on the subject of Smith and the tragedy into which he had slipped. Those present included people from the community, as well as other prisoners and some of Smith's relatives from Ansonia. When Father McGivney shakily asked for their prayers on his own behalf, he drew tears from those who knew him from St. Mary's and who were used to seeing him laughing and making grand plans for the future.[15] McGivney's remarks that day were transcribed by a reporter, who noted that the priest's voice was "broken with emotion" as he addressed the people in attendance:

Our gathering this morning is on a very solemn occasion. The service has been held expressly for the benefit of one individual. Under the circumstances I shall say but a very few words and detain you but a moment or two, that more time may be devoted to that one of whom I have spoken. I am requested by Mr. Smith to ask pardon for all faults he may have had and all offences he may have committed, and at his request I ask for the prayers of all of you, that when next Friday comes he may die a holy death. In saying that he does not care to live longer, I am using his words. This resignation on his part shows that he is prepared for what is to come in a few days. I trust that all of you will offer up fervent prayer to the throne of grace that God will strengthen and prepare us to perform that awful duty which we shall be called upon to perform before this time next Sunday.

To me this duty comes with almost a crushing weight. If I could consistently with my duty be far away from here next Friday I should escape perhaps the most trying ordeal of my life, but this sad duty is placed my way by providence and must be fulfilled. If we receive your prayers, Mr. Smith and I shall be sustained by the supreme power in the hour of our great trial. I once again ask forgiveness for all the wrong doing of which he has been guilty. He forgives all from the bottom of his heart, and I ask you for the aid of your prayers that he may be fully prepared for a happy death.[16]

Father McGivney spent much of each day with Smith during the last week. No one else was admitted to the cell without written permission from the priest.[17] Late in the afternoon on the day before the hanging, Smith's mother and sister came to say good-bye for the last time. As they left, dissolved in tears, "even Rev. Father McGivney broke down," according to a report in the *Union*. McGivney left just before midnight. Word went through the jail that after that the condemned man slept "as peacefully and quietly as a child."[18]

The next morning, Smith was awakened by Constable Daniel Colwell (who also happened to be one of the founding members of the Knights of Columbus). Smith thanked Colwell for his many kindnesses. He promised to think of him when he was in heaven. Father McGivney arrived soon after, greeted Smith warmly, and repaired with him to another room for morning Mass. At ten thirty, they were on the gallows, Father McGivney—described as "devout but quite calm"—reading prayers and Chip repeating them in a whisper. Then the execution took place.

Smith left his possessions, including many religious items, to various relatives and friends. To Father McGivney, who had given him hope, he left the "plant now blooming in my cell." More than that, he left McGivney with the tribute of his parting words to his mother, the day before the hanging. Seeing her crying uncontrollably, he threw his arms around her and exclaimed, "Mother, don't cry for me! I will soon be better off. Just think if I had been shot that night and died without a moment's time for preparation, how much worse off I should be than I am now. I have asked God to forgive me my sins and believe that I shall die a happy death."[19] That Smith reached that point, after starting such a long way from it, was the work of the priest who had stood beside him. It was the essence of the work of every parish priest.

11

INERTIA IN A HURRY

"Father McGivney did not recover from the strain for some time," recalled Cornelius Driscoll and William Geary, speaking of the Chip Smith ordeal.[1] At the age of thirty, McGivney was badly in need of a rest, but that didn't mean that he was able to take one. The lack of progress in the development of the Knights of Columbus weighed on him constantly. He had poured everything he knew into the fraternal organization, including his commitment to the Church and his firsthand understanding of the frail state of finance in most families.

Nonetheless, a few of his fellow priests disapproved of the new organization. The idea that the assistant pastor of the most debt-ridden church in the diocese had dreams of a huge financial organization made McGivney seem like an overambitious upstart to some people in the Church. The mere thought that he would somehow preside over this statewide group—a shadow bishop with his own power base—made a number of his more suspicious colleagues openly wary of him and his grandiose plans. Those who knew Father McGivney, however, were aware that his ambitions were entirely selfless. Father Lawlor and Bishop McMahon were both solidly behind his effort to bring the Knights of Columbus to fruition. Yet even their encouragement was a burden of sorts: the thought of squandering their trust in a failure gave Father McGivney yet another worry as 1882 settled into its final months, and the Knights of Columbus still showed no progress.

Each day, McGivney faced Catholic families with troubles that might have been avoided with the support of the Knights of Columbus. The longer it remained invisible, if not downright illusory, the longer those families were without hope.

"In New Haven, today," read a report at the time, "there are not a few children of Irish birth who need help, moral as well as physical help. Hundreds of Irish youth of both sexes are growing up in our midst, in abject poverty, in filth, wretchedness and crime for want of help and sympathy."[2] The Knights of Columbus could not be expected to remedy every case, but the organization was Father McGivney's best response to the scenes he witnessed every day. It would be his weapon against the threat of sudden poverty for families already bereaved.

As September began, the organization was going in the wrong direction and the pressures building within the Knights of Columbus were set to erupt. For the time being, the central administration (the Supreme Council) and the sole chapter in

New Haven were largely one and the same, with virtually the same leadership. The New Haven chapter, or "council," had named itself San Salvador, after the first island that Columbus reached in the New World.

All of the Knights were friends of Father McGivney, or so he thought. One of those to whom he was especially close was Michael Curran, New Haven's only Catholic undertaker and the treasurer of the struggling Knights.

Curran's daughter, Jane, became acquainted with most of the founders of the Knights of Columbus, and she later re-called the frustration they all felt as the group stalled in 1882. One of her specific recollections concerned Bart Healy, a thirty-year-old shop clerk who had been on the original committee of twelve. "At one of the meetings, Bart Healy said, after a quarrel over something, that he never knew a so-ciety to prosper which had a priest at its head," Jane Curran related. "That evening Healy and some others drew right out." They simply announced that they had quit, and then left. The timing of such a personal attack couldn't have been worse for Michael McGivney, who was still worn from the strain of the summer and the final months of the Chip Smith ordeal.

"Next day," Miss Curran continued, "Father McGivney wanted to pull out himself, if it was true that he was not a good influence for, or asset to, the Order." Both Michael Cur-ran and his wife were incensed at Healy's action.[3] Nor were they ameliorated when Healy and his followers returned to the Knights after a short time. For McGivney, however, it was enough that they were back. The Knights of Columbus was the cause closest to his heart. He had no real choice in any decision but to try to keep the group together and moving forward.

During September, several meetings were held in response to the rather dire lack of new members. "Although many eligible men had been solicited to become members of San Salvador #1," Driscoll and Geary later remembered, "none had accepted and interest had begun to waiver so much that at a meeting of the Council in September, just six months after the institution of the order, a Committee was appointed by the Grand Knight to confer with the Chief Ranger of the A.O. Forresters [*sic*], as to forming the members of the Council into a new court of Forresters. If that would be done the Charter of San Salvador would be surrendered."[4]

Nothing could have been worse, from Father McGivney's point of view. The Ancient Order of Foresters was not the *Catholic* Foresters, that Massachusetts version of a secret society that had already turned the New Haven group away. The Ancient Order of Foresters was the supposedly nondenominational organization that, in the view of the Church, offered a kind of ersatz refuge to men of all religions. As far as Michael McGivney was concerned, it created nothing better in the lives of its Catholic members than a faint pressure to let their faith lapse.

Perhaps Father McGivney was overly sensitive where the Foresters were concerned. All it was, really, was a men's club with a benevolent insurance plan attached. To McGivney, however, what made it evil in the lives of Catholics lay in what the organization wasn't. It wasn't a continuing source of support in putting a man in touch with family: his own family as well as the Holy Family. The Catholic Foresters, and even more so the Knights of Columbus, sought to give such a man a firm place in the evolving universe of modern life. Membership in the Knights made a man a hero—but not for hunting, pioneering, or cutting down trees in order to provide for his family. There was nothing of the fantasy about its underlying mission. Unfortunately, at the September meeting, Father McGivney was voted down on the subject of seeking out the mantle of another secret society.

A committee of three men looked into the possibility of reorganizing the Knights of Columbus as a "court" of Foresters. During late September and early October, McGivney awaited their report with foreboding. He was the only one who seemed to realize how much was about to be lost.

Then the Foresters, his bête noire, did Father McGivney the greatest possible favor. As Driscoll and Geary related: "The committee reported on a Sunday afternoon . . . that they had conferred with the Chief Ranger, as to his forming a new court of Foresters, to be composed of the members of San Salvador Council. The Chief Ranger declined to form a new court."

The chief ranger countered that the Knights could spread themselves out among the four courts already operating in New Haven.[5] The Knights who had gathered to hear the report on the Foresters were not idiots. It immediately occurred to them that the reason they were being turned down was that they were all Catholics. (In fairness to the Foresters, it is probable that they didn't want any courts that were restricted by religious affiliation, whether it was to be a Roman Catholic court or a Presbyterian, Baptist, or Jewish one.)

For a Catholic in the United States in the late nineteenth century, though, any rejection on religious grounds hurt with a special sting, especially for those who were determined to prove themselves in a country still predominantly Protestant. Even the most evenhanded Protestants couldn't help but notice that the Catholic population of the country was rising dramatically. In 1830, there were 318,000 Catholics in the United States, accounting for about 3 percent of the total population.[6] In 1870, there were 3,555,000, and that number doubled in just ten years, so that by 1880, Catholics represented 12 percent of the population.[7]

For Catholics, the suspicion remained that the anti-Catholic vendetta of the 1850s—the Know-Nothing uprising—was only barely submerged beneath a thin layer of goodwill. Even in the enlightened year of 1880, an erudite magazine like *The International Review* contended that in line with Catholic teachings, soldiers would desert their posts to go to confession, doctors would commit fraud, and people of all stripes would overlook sin if it led to some advantage: "It is clear that these teachings are not in accord with American ideas of the Christian morality."[8] Such articles were common, as were their fallacies regarding Roman Catholics and the Catholic religion. *The Unitarian Review* was a little more careful with its facts, but there was high-toned prejudice in its suggestion that "the considerate and fair-minded among the priesthood will not grudge the making of some allowances to the shock, or at least the strain, to which in many parts of New England the descendants of the original English stock have been subjected by the crowding in upon them during the last fifty years of members of the Roman Church."[9]

Whether blatant or veiled, anti-Catholic sentiments were acceptable in 1880, and the men who gathered to start the group that Father McGivney envisioned were all familiar with the bias against them, and the ache it left. Quiet anti-Catholic prejudice formed part of the backdrop against which Father McGivney called New Haven's brightest Catholic men together, and in part they formed their group—quietly—as a response to it.

At the October meeting, the sixteen men who had gathered to hear the report on the application to the Foresters suddenly bounced back from their initial disappointment. All at once, they rallied around Father McGivney, like small children who had changed their minds about running away from home. Geary and Driscoll recalled the mood of the committee members as the meeting ended: "We will not surrender our Charter. We will not humiliate the Founder [Father McGivney] and his associates."[10]

The Knights left the meeting absolutely determined to save the order. But then the next day rolled around. Cornelius Driscoll had recently accepted the prestigious position of corporation counsel for the city of New Haven. William Geary was getting ready to open a new grocery store in downtown New Haven.[11] And James Mullen had got himself engaged. The founding members were very busy, as usual, and so they didn't accomplish anything in late 1882.

Along with other people in New Haven, McGivney read a well-publicized report on the county's poor children when it was issued that same October. Commissioned by the governor's office and written by a teacher named Wight at the Yale Divinity School, it concluded that there were two primary causes for the plight of impoverished children.

In all of the county's cities, Wight wrote, specifically citing New Haven and Meriden, "you will find many widows with from three to nine children each, who are struggling along in the hopeless endeavor to properly support themselves and families. . . . Competition is too close, wages too small and manual labor too inefficient to enable these women to succeed in their worthy effort to keep their families from suffering, uneducated and handicapped as they all are."

In comments directed at the governor, Wight asserted, "What can be done for the relief of such families is, it seems to me, a problem for your commission to solve." Father McGivney knew perfectly well that the Knights of Columbus could offer an answer, except that it wasn't yet operational. Any government program was bound to be only a partial answer, anyway, because it could address only the physical needs of the children. "Food and shelter," Wight wrote, speaking of government institutions for poor children, "will save a child from physical death, but the influences of pauperism will deaden pride and ambition, which latter among the poorer classes amounts to hope and without these incentives to activity, man becomes spiritually dead." That was precisely why Michael McGivney had designed his Knights as more than merely a benevolent program.

Wight's second conclusion might well have been McGivney's, too. The professor continued:

> Another great evil that has come to my notice, especially in the cities, is the desertion of their children by fathers. In one city, one-sixth of the cases reported come under this head. The man who brings into the

world innocent children is responsible before God and man for their upbringing in an age which will warrant their looking out for themselves, and the father who deserts his family becomes answerable to the public and should be made to feel the guilt of his action.[12]

According to Wight's report, the problem of child poverty stemmed largely from the fathers. Either they died, which was hardly their own fault, or else they deserted. And that might not have been their fault, either, inasmuch as they might not have known much better. Many men, as Father McGivney knew full well, had a lot to learn about how to be a husband and father. But as the months dragged by for him, the problems were not merely statistics. They were the people at his door asking for help.

Throughout late 1882, Michael McGivney continued to work on behalf of the Knights of Columbus and, of course, St. Mary's. The big news of the early autumn at the church was that Thomas Fitzgerald had recovered enough from his bout with insanity to return and resume his position as organist at St. Mary's. In late autumn, Father Lawlor was bedridden with a severe lung condition. After he recovered, he was more delicate than ever, walking with the measured steps of a much older man.

James Splain had been feeling better since his return to New Haven, and Father McGivney was cheered by his company. Many of Splain's friends, in fact, forgot entirely that he had been sick, and started wondering when he would renew his medical practice. Splain probably knew better. Over the winter, his tuberculosis returned and confined him to a sick-room in his mother's house. Father McGivney was described as a "constant attendant at the bedside," trying to keep his friend's spirits up, often with humor, just as Splain had done for him at Our Lady of Angels. During early March, however, Splain was in "excruciating agony," according to a report that reached the newspaper. On Saturday, March 10, just as the noon chimes were ringing over the city, James Splain died. "Genial, companionable and sociable, with a ready wit that gleamed even through his hours of sickness, he won friends wherever he went," declared the *New Haven Morning Journal and Courier.* Father McGivney officiated at the funeral, speaking with great feeling of his remarkable friend.[13]

Tuberculosis was the leading cause of death in the late nineteenth century. Until 1882, the year before Splain's death, no one even knew what caused it or that it was spread by bacteria that shot into the air every time a TB victim coughed. What practically everyone in those days did know all too well was who among their friends had died of TB. In Connecticut, it claimed roughly twice as many victims as the second-most common cause of death, pneumonia.[14] TB could take anyone, but it preyed on young and middle-aged adults, especially those worn from fatigue or tension.

Following pneumonia, which was often associated with alcoholism in the nineteenth century, the other leading causes of death in Connecticut were "old age," cholera, and heart disease. Aside from old age, all could target people otherwise considered in the prime of life. Those were the situations into which Father McGivney walked every day, while Driscoll and Mullen, Geary and Colwell and all the other Knights let a whole year go by. They each had to see to more pressing matters.

In January 1883, a workman named Michael Moran left his job in the roundhouse of the Consolidated Railroad with a stabbing pain in his side. He had been under treatment for heart disease, but he didn't think that was the problem. On coming home, he told his wife he just wanted to rest. The next day, he died of heart failure. That left his wife with four children and no money whatsoever.[15]

In February, a widow named Ann Moran—no relation to Michael—was in a state of utter poverty, trying to take care of her one-year-old baby with no income at all, except the tiny amount she received from the city in alms. On a Sunday morning, her baby died of starvation. Sometime later a doctor arrived, but only to sign a death certificate. On Monday, all alone, the mother carried the baby's body to the Catholic cemetery. She didn't have the money for a casket, or even for the interment. "The sexton took compassion on her," according to a report, "and buried it."[16]

12

FAITH IN MERIDEN

It was hard to tell what was what at St. Mary's in the early spring of 1883.

The bad news, which was that Thomas Fitzgerald suddenly quit as organist, started to seem like good news once Father McGivney had a chance to think about it. Fitzgerald, in his manic way, had not informed anyone that he was quitting; he just hopped on a train, leaving word only that he had taken another job in an unnamed city.

Likewise, the good news—that a group of men in the town of Meriden wanted to organize a Knights of Columbus council—started to seem like bad news, once the initial flush of excitement had passed. McGivney had brought the latest dilemma on himself with his success as a press agent; the people in Meriden learned about the new Catholic order in an article carried in the *Boston Pilot,* a weekly devoted to Catholic and Irish-American news in New England. Mc-Givney simply didn't know what to say to them. He didn't necessarily want to betray the fact that the Knights of Columbus were still in disarray. In addition, the town of Meriden was the home turf of Father Thomas Walsh, who had made it known within the diocese that he did not approve of fighting nondenominational secret societies with Catholic ones. Even if Father McGivney had been in a position to send detailed information on forming a new council (which he was not), he was daunted by the idea of reaching out to any Catholic in Meriden without raising the ire of Father Walsh. In that, Walsh was not unlike West Peak, the tall mountain that loomed over the city; both of them, immutable, watched over everything that happened in Meriden.

One of the organizers in Meriden was a man named George O'Connor, who wrote his own account of the initial efforts in 1895. His writing style was rustic, as he recalled the view of the situation from the other side:

> At this time [early 1883] two men in Meriden Geo O'Connor & P. J. Ford in conversation lamented the condition in which so many of our people were when the Head of the House Died. Depending on the cold charity of the World. P. J. Ford told Geo O'Connor that he had seen a peice [*sic*] in the *Boston Pilot* about some Priest that was trying to organize a Society that would give One Thousand Dollars at the Death of a member. Geo O'Connor told P. J. Ford to hunt up the paper. He did so and Geo O'Connor

told P. J. Ford to write to New Haven and get all particulars.[1]

When Father McGivney received Ford's letter from Meriden, he was surprised and very pleased with the new situation, at least at first. He sent a reply that showed that his belief in the new order was, if anything, stronger than ever:

> Oweing [*sic*] to my absence from the City yesterday I could not answer sooner. I am glad to know that Meriden's Catholic Young Men are not behind the age in looking for their own benefit. Herewith I send you copies of our By-Laws &c. After perusing them I hope you will come to the conclusion of forming a council in Meriden.
>
> You will see that when we are well established in the diocese we can bid defiance to the secret societies & bring our fellow catholics to enjoy without any danger to their faith all the benefits which those societies offer as an inducement to enter them. When you answer please tell me the date of the *Pilot* in which you saw the notice about our order. After you read the By Laws & answer I will give you all the information necessary for the formation of a Council in Meriden.[2]

Father McGivney's letter galvanized the spirit of the men in Meriden. Without delay, they called a general meeting to share the materials sent by the priest. As O'Connor wrote, "The Constution [*sic*] and Papers & Blanks were read by Geo O'Connor, after which one man made a motion that we invite the officers to come to Meriden and explain it as it would take a Phyladelphia [*sic*] Lawyer to understand it."

O'Connor continued, "That was a block in our way, as we found that the New Haven People were in a kind of a trance which we found hard to awaken them from."[3] P. J. Ford peppered McGivney and the other Knights of Columbus in New Haven with more letters and a few telegrams. Each time, he went to O'Connor for the stationery—and the stamp. All Ford contributed was the ink. That rankled O'Connor considerably, but no organization is launched without each person in it revealing one annoying characteristic or another. The one thing that annoyed all of the candidate Knights in Meriden was the response they were receiving, or not receiving, from Michael McGivney. They assumed that, after the notice he had posted in the *Boston Pilot,* he would jump all over their interest in his order. To their dismay, he seemed for all the world to be stalling. He wasn't, at least not of his own volition. But he was caught in a diplomatic quandary that threatened an early end to the Knights of Columbus if he made a wrong move.

Finally, P. J. Ford wrote Father McGivney on April 17 and mentioned that the Meriden group was looking into the possibility of joining the Ancient Order of Foresters. That did it. McGivney wrote back the same day—twice.

And he explained the delay in his previous correspondence:

> Your dispatch this morning occasioned both joy and sorrow. Joy at the thoughts of you being so anxious to form a council & sorrow to hear that you had it in mind to join the Forresters [*sic*] which I

hope you will never do. I sent a dispatch this morning
and one to-night. I hope that you have not acted one
way or the other yet. You know that one cause of delay & I may say the principal one was my waiting for a
letter from Fr. Walsh, not receiving it I had to get to
work & prepare one of the other members of the
Supreme Council to go to Meriden and I was about to
telegraph to-night to say a delegation of two would
go up to Meriden & organize but unfortunately I am
held in suspense by the sickness of his wife—

I would willingly go myself, but you know that if
I did Fr. Walsh would come out against the Order &
destroy all our hopes. So I came to the conclusion that
it was better for me to send a delegate, as the order is
purely civil & business like in all its transactions. Now
Mr. Ford if you and the young men in Meriden
intending to join our band will be a little patient I
promise you everything will come out satisfactorily.[4]

Two days later, in the midst of the pressure to do something about Meriden, Father McGivney was suddenly called to
New Britain, about thirty miles north of New Haven on the
way to Hartford. His train passed through Meriden and he
could spot the twin towers of St. Rose's, Father Walsh's
church, rising near the middle of the small city. McGivney
could not linger over his problems with Meriden, however. He
was on another type of business, and a mission he didn't relish.

That morning, Father Hugh Carmody had been found lying unconscious near the bottom of the staircase in the front
hall of his residence in New Britain. Father McGivney and a

physician named Bacon from New Haven were immediately summoned. As McGivney learned, a lamplighting device had been lying near Father Carmody's hand; apparently, he had been leaning over the railing, midway up the staircase, trying to light a gaslight in the front hall, when he fell over the railing, dropping about five feet and hitting his head on a post as he fell.[5]

When Father McGivney arrived at midday on Friday, Carmody was still unconscious. Late in the evening, he woke up just enough to recognize his young friend from New Haven.[6] Dr. Bacon examined the wounds to Carmody's head and ascertained that there was no chance of recovery. As Father Carmody's life ebbed over the weekend, hourly reports were sent to New Haven, where his legion of former parishioners at St. John's anguished.[7] McGivney stayed with Carmody during most of the last hours and was with him on Monday morning when he died.

All of New Britain prepared for the funeral, the civic officials predicting that it would draw more people than any other event in the history of the town. Among those who would work together on the preparations were the Reverend Michael McGivney of New Haven and the Reverend Thomas Walsh of Meriden.

In the evening on that same Monday, a delegation of three Knights, including John Kerrigan, William Sellwood, and J. T. McMahon, also traveled north, to meet with the Meriden contingent.[8] "Finaly [sic]," acknowledged George O'Connor, "we got Bros Kerrigan McMahon & Sellwood to come to Meriden and explain the merits of the Order."

O'Connor noted dryly, "They did not tell us at that time

the condition they were in N. Haven." But that no longer mattered: the men in Meriden took up the Knights of Columbus idea with their own zeal. In that, they soon found that Father McGivney was right to regard Father Walsh with trepidation, as O'Connor explained:

> The first thing was to get a Chaplain. George O'Connor was delegated to wait on the Pastor of St. Roses [*sic*] then Vicar General [Father Walsh]. He did so, laid the Constitution & Papers before him. After half an hours talk he [O'Connor] had to leave his mission having failed as the Rev Vicar General was opposed to such a Society. This was a serious Block as we could not start without a Catholic Priest as Chaplain.

Father McGivney heard about the outcome of the meeting with Father Walsh. For the first time in the short history of his Knights of Columbus, he was absolutely powerless. Any intimation that he was meddling in Walsh's parish decisions would be unseemly at best, and disastrous in any case to the goal of starting a council in Meriden.

Back in Meriden, George O'Connor and P. J. Ford considered their options. "We resorted to . . . Bro Dolbec to see what he could do with Father Van Oppen," O'Connor wrote.[9] David Dolbec, a bookkeeper by profession, was a member of Meriden's French-Canadian community. As part of the ongoing effort of the diocese to cater to the needs of various immigrant contingents, a French-language church called St. Laurent's had been organized in Meriden in 1880. The pastor was Alphonse Van Oppen, a native of Belgium.[10] The prospective Knights set their sights on him.

"After some time and trouble," O'Connor wrote, "Father Van Oppen consented to become a member and Chaplain, and I must say that if we had not succeeded with Father Van Oppen at that time the K of C would not be in existence today." O'Connor might have been right about that.

The organizers in Meriden immediately started recruiting potential members, who were duly scrutinized by an investigating committee. Those organizers may have been silver burnishers, polishers, and clerks by vocation, but they had an innate understanding of the insurance business: they wanted only healthy men for their plan. George O'Connor, who was head of the investigating committee, took pride in the fact that the doctor didn't have to reject anyone who was sent to him. The committee used its own intelligence-gathering methods to evaluate the candidates, and those in less than excellent condition never made it as far as the examining physician.[11]

Within a month, the Meriden group had thirty-two carefully vetted men who were ready to be initiated as Knights of Columbus. After consultation with the Supreme Council in New Haven, the installation ceremony was scheduled for May 16. Just before that night arrived, Father Walsh issued an edict that no one from his parish, St. Rose's, could join the Knights of Columbus. The original thirty-two members remained loyal to the group, but further recruitment, except from St. Laurent's Church, practically ground to a halt.

With a kind of desperation, a detail of officers from New Haven took the train to Meriden on May 16. And with the same kind of desperation, the thirty-two men from Meriden prepared to greet them. George O'Connor's wife and a silver-worker named John Dowling sewed regalia for the event, according to patterns of their own design.

James Mullen took it upon himself to direct the installation ceremonies in Meriden, assisted by John Kerrigan. William Sellwood, J. T. McMahon, and Daniel Colwell also made the trip to Meriden. Father McGivney, the founder of the order, stayed home in New Haven, despite the fact that the initiation of the new council probably meant more to him than to anyone who would be there. A second council represented just the prod he needed in order to wake up the core Knights in New Haven and get them moving forward. Nonetheless, McGivney was too savvy to show his face in Meriden. Sitting in the study of the rectory that night, he could at least console himself that things were happening: with or without him, his plan was working.

The five Knights from New Haven who did make the trip apparently impressed the Meriden group, but only at first. "We had from N.H. all of the officers," wrote George O'Connor, "who went thro a very strange Initiation & Instalation form got up for the occasion . . . for they had neither Initiation or Instalation forms [in advance]. No ritual whatsoever. They got thro in a manner they have often laughed over since."[12]

The initiation of the 12,000th council of the Knights of Columbus in 2003 would not prove the worth of Michael McGivney's original idea more soundly than had the formation of

Silver City Council #2, in Meriden. Previously, the insiders in New Haven hadn't recognized what a powerful resource they had, no matter how hard Father McGivney tried to convince them. It was the imperative of the outsiders, the men in Meriden, that gave the Knights in New Haven no choice but to react. After that, having accepted the compliment of imitation from Meriden, the Knights in New Haven also finally accepted the responsibility of operating the order in a manner that was, as Father McGivney put it, purely "business like in all its transactions."

McGivney's dream was realized at that very significant, if bewildering, ceremony in Meriden. Men from different parishes were united in a Catholic society designed to help them in the Christian obligation, and the modern heroism, of caring for a family, spiritually and financially.

13

A STERN VOICE

On March 26, 1883, customers at the Downes Literary Emporium seemed to be taking unusual interest in an out-of-town newspaper called the *New London Day*. Long before the afternoon came to an end, Edward Downes Jr. noticed that the stack that had arrived that morning was gone, dwindled right down to the bare floor. New London, a small city about fifty miles east of New Haven, was curious enough about the news and incident of New Haven to pay a correspondent there for tidbits. The edition of March 26 contained an especially delectable one:

> Much gossip is occasioned among the members
> of St. Mary's Catholic congregation by the quite reg-
> ular appearance among them of a daughter of one of

our prominent Episcopal clergymen. This young lady, who is amiable and rarely accomplished and moves in the best society, unites in the devotions. On Easter Sunday, she was at early mass and united in all except in going forward to the alter [*sic*] to receive communion. The Catholics think she is fairly on the way to conversion to the tenets.[1]

The same item was picked up in the New Haven papers the next day, and once it was, the story raced through both religious and social circles. For those who speculated on the identity of the "prominent Episcopal clergyman," the list narrowed quickly down to one obvious and yet spectacular choice.

The Rev. Dr. Edwin Harwood of Trinity Church was fairly brittle with prominence, a man so very social that he could make it known that he preferred the isolation of his study, so very pious that he could leave the sermons and the services to others, and so widely respected that the trustees of Trinity Church could repeatedly try to edge him out, and never even come close to succeeding.[2] In Episcopalian circles, Harwood was known as the founder of the Protestant Episcopal Church Congress, an annual meeting of clergymen from throughout the country. In view of its importance, Harwood liked to call the chapel in Trinity Church "the cradle of the Congress." The only dream he had remaining for that congress was someday hosting it in New Haven.

Marion Harwood was more social than her husband, having come from a family of considerable stature in Hempstead, across the Sound from New Haven on New York's Long Island.

Together, the couple raised six children in the Trinity rectory, which was located downtown just a few blocks from the New Haven Green. Every time one of the children so much as took a walk unchaperoned, people noticed and took it up in discussion all over town. Perhaps that explains why James, the oldest son, didn't follow in his father's footsteps. Or anyone else's: he moved to Fort Assiniboine, Montana—a place that might be described succinctly as the very antithesis of the Green in New Haven, Connecticut. He worked as a wilderness guide.[3] As of 1883, the other two surviving Harwood children were living at home.

Since they were both young women, it was a little frustrating at first for New Haven gossips to discern just which one was sneaking out to St. Mary's Church. Alida, at twenty-two, and Honora, twenty, were both "amiable," as the *New London Day* had indicated in its description, and both moved "in the best society." Both also happened to be regarded as belles in New Haven. Alida, however, was clearly the one who was "rarely accomplished," often singing or playing piano at recitals. And it was indeed Alida who had started attending St. Mary's, drawn there initially by her maid.

Alida Harwood soon formed a friendship with Father McGivney, in whom she found a "firm spiritual friend and advisor," according to another newspaper report. McGivney delighted in her interest in the Church and he couldn't help but be impressed at her erudition. Just to grow up in Dr. Harwood's house was to enjoy an advanced classical education. Alida, described as "beautiful, with a singular grace of manner and sweetness of disposition," certainly knew her Bible and was a careful student of Christian history.[4]

Michael McGivney treated Alida Harwood as he would any other visitor to his church. While he was appealingly and absolutely certain in his own convictions, he was not a man to put pressure on a potential convert. A parish priest did not typically lean forward to "sell" the Church, anyway, but only remain upright, a particularly stable beacon in any community. McGivney was nevertheless sensitive to Alida's background. He knew that it took courage for Edwin Harwood's daughter to set foot inside St. Mary's. Out of respect for her position, he didn't do anything to draw attention to her participation in the celebration of Mass. The article in the *New London Day* came as a shock to him.

It was an even bigger shock to Dr. Harwood, who hadn't realized just how far Alida's visits to St. Mary's had gone. A week later, to show that all was well, he scheduled a performance by his daughter at English Hall, the building used for Episcopal functions in New Haven. She led off with "Jesus and It Shall Ever Be," and also sang "There Is a Green Hill Far Away."[5] That stopped the gossip for the moment, or at least made it more serpentine, but there was still turmoil in the rectory.

Harwood told some of his parishioners that he was going to resign and devote the rest of his life to literary studies.[6] Eventually, however, he decided to stay in his pulpit. In the meantime, Alida was packed off to Europe with her mother and sister.[7] She was supposed to work on getting over her fascination with Catholicism and forget her conversations with Father McGivney.

Even before Alida left for Europe, David Hillhouse Buel graduated from Yale with the class of '83: another young person with news for Father McGivney. Buel had decided that he wanted to become a priest.

McGivney had been David Buel's first friend within the Church and the young man's conversion was "due to God's grace in Father McGivney," as the Reverend Joseph Daley later told it.[8] For better or worse, however, Buel was a youth of raging enthusiasms. His inclination toward the priesthood had to come from something deeper than that. The best plan, and the one endorsed by Father McGivney, was for Buel to reserve his final decision until he had time for unhurried contemplation. Only with reflection and prayer would he know his rightful place in the Church. Buel tended to be impatient, but he accepted the fact that he ought to pause and confirm the verity of his calling. To that end, he made plans to spend the summer traveling in Canada.[9]

Just as the summer began, Michael McGivney was forced by circumstance to resume the position of treasurer of the St. Joseph's Young Men's Total Abstinence and Literary Society. The group had become, sadly enough, much too successful. Control of it was important enough to fight over and a couple of different factions were willing to tear it apart in the process.

Every show the TAL put on was met by a full house, every review was glowing. Young women had become an integral part of the shows, however, and the old guard in the parish believed that the group needed closer supervision. The leadership seemed to be fraying. Under some pressure from the church authorities—meaning Fathers Lawlor and McGivney—the members voted in a new slate of officers, including McGivney.

Not everyone liked the new officers or the intimation that the club had been in some sense wayward. A whole battalion of members resigned in protest, certain that the fun was all out of the TAL.

By the first day of August, the TAL had stabilized enough to schedule an excursion by steamboat to Coney Island, the famous beach in New York City. The club's cursed good luck continued: more people wanted to go than could fit onboard, leading to pandemonium at the dock.[10] Finally, the steamship got under way, with twelve hundred paying passengers. Father McGivney, as treasurer and chaplain, had to oversee both the finances of the day and the well-being of all the people who rode the mechanical rides and ate too much candy. Coney Island being what it is, that was probably all twelve hundred.

The only people who were not happy with the success of the rather ambitious excursion were the ex-members of the TAL. They stayed home, where there was little to do except grow even more disgruntled. In time, they planned an excursion of their own, renting two barges from Smedley's boatyard to take themselves and as many young women as cared to join them to a secluded park called South End Grove—unchaperoned. To help ensure that young women of quality would be disposed to join the excursion, the organizers let it be known, or let it be assumed, that St. Joseph's TAL was the sponsor of the outing. That fallacy was printed in the Saturday newspapers, in a general invitation to join the excursion. When Father McGivney read the item, he was incensed. It was too late to go to the newspapers for a correction—the barges were due to leave the following afternoon. The newspapers didn't matter with him anyway; he took his response directly to his parishioners.

After nine o'clock Mass on the day of the "South End affair," as it was later called, McGivney grew as angry as any of his parishioners had ever seen him. According to a person who was there:

> Father McGivney denounced from the altar the young men who were to take part in the South End affair, and with much emphasis pointed out that they had no connection with the St. Joseph's society and that the society was in nowise responsible for whatever might happen at the picnic. He dwelt on the lack of religious spirit manifested by the participants in the picnic, and said that immeasurable scandal would be given by having well known young Catholics traversing in pairs in the woods about South End on a Sunday afternoon.[11]

The rebellious ex-members heard about Father McGivney's denunciation that morning and held a discussion on whether or not to proceed with their adventure. When the talking was through, they boarded the barges with their girls and floated down to South End. But they might as well have been chaperoned, knowing as they did that the priests at St. Mary's were ready to scrutinize their behavior. The outing was itself uneventful.

St. Joseph's TAL quieted down, but as autumn approached, Father McGivney's main distraction outside of church, the Knights of Columbus, was gathering new momentum.

The robust growth of Meriden's Silver City Council encouraged men in other parts of the state to recognize the potential of the order. Father McGivney personally visited small
cities and towns such as Middletown, Norwalk, and Thomaston, each of which sought to establish councils of their own
in autumn of 1883.[12] In Thomaston, with a population of just
two thousand, the Catholic priest was Father Eugene Gaffney.
As a friend of Father McGivney, he promoted the idea of a
council with extra enthusiasm.

Alida Harwood returned from Europe after the summer
with her mother and sister, Honora. The trip had done her
good, in a spiritual way—or at least she thought so. She came
back more resolved than ever to immerse herself into the
Catholic faith and lost no time in returning to St. Mary's for
the regular services and the abiding counsel of Father Michael
McGivney. Dr. Harwood, for his part, went off to his Protestant Episcopal Church Congress in Philadelphia during the
first week of October, while Alida stayed in New Haven and
quietly attended solemn vespers at a special Sunday night service at St. Mary's. "Father McGivney," the local press reported, "delivered a short but impressive sermon on the
divine maternity of Mary and the power she wields at the
throne of grace, which should be invoked by prayerful
Catholics."[13]

Not long afterward, *Penikeese* was in rehearsal for yet another production in New Haven, but its librettist was not to be
found scribbling notes for new lyrics in the balcony.[14] David
Buel was far away from the world of Cuisine and Cupid,
studying instead for the priesthood with the Society of Jesus
in West Park, New York. He was contented in his faith for the

moment, but Alida Harwood, as Father McGivney knew first-hand, was still struggling with her future.

When the lead soprano of Trinity Church in New Haven retired, Alida's name surfaced as the probable replacement.[15] She was a logical choice, inasmuch as she had a trained voice that parishioners were used to hearing at Trinity events. A generous soul, she had yet to stop appearing at special fund-raisers and other recitals for the church. Anyway, she was still duly intimidated by her father. But she just didn't see how she could sing at Trinity on Sunday mornings and simultaneously worship at St. Mary's, a half mile away. In early May 1884, an-other soprano was engaged for the Trinity choir.[16]

The same week, Father McGivney decided to speak up about his own choir, which apparently could have used Miss Harwood. During his regular announcements after the last Mass, he acknowledged the choir rather tepidly and then cited the members for their "careless and irregular attendance at re-hearsals." In his opinion, however, the real cause of the poor performance of the choir lay with those people who were sneaking up to the gallery, getting in the way and standing there "like statues," while the others sang. McGivney sus-pected that those who were invading the choir space were es-caping the obligation to pay rent for space in the pews downstairs. In view of the fact that the previous December both he and Father Lawlor had donated the entire Christmas collection (intended for their personal use) to defray the church debt, such stinginess was a sore point.[17]

Michael McGivney's spontaneous criticism sparked a bil-low of controversy at St. Mary's. The so-called statues de-clared themselves injured. Members of the choir said they were miffed. Anything related to a choir is apt to touch sensitive feelings, but the response to McGivney's comments was particularly pithy. "It is hoped that with the absence of the statues," stated a parishioner in an article in the *New Haven Morning Journal and Courier,* "the choir may receive a sudden quickening of vocal enthusiasm and excellence that will be a desired improvement on the ragged work that has of late offended the delicate musical tastes of the clergyman."[18]

The following week, the interlopers were gone from the gallery, but some of the choir singers were said to be gone, too, in a sort of sympathy strike. The *New Haven Union* sent a reporter to the rectory on Monday afternoon to see whether Father McGivney had considered delivering any retraction of his criticism, as it had been reported in the previous week's *Morning Journal and Courier.* "Fathers Lawlor and McGivney sat in the parlor of their residence," the *Union* writer noted:

> They did not look as though they were greatly disturbed by what had been published concerning the latter's remarks a week ago. Father McGivney had not even taken the trouble to read the paper to see what had been published. When he did read it, he said: "That is very malicious and I think arises from the fact that there has been such silence observed on our part. No sir, I don't intend to say anything more about the matter. The statement is not true that some of our leading solists [*sic*] did not sing yesterday because of what I said. It is something like what was stated in last Monday's [*Morning Journal and Courier*]. There were three misstatements in last Monday's paper. Every

singer who belongs in our choir was there yesterday unless excused.[19]

The "statues" controversy, along with the previous summer's South End affair, showed the parishioners at St. Mary's a new side of Michael McGivney. He was still the approachable and optimistic man they had always known, but at thirty-one, he had developed enough of a sense of perspective to express displeasure when he felt it strongly enough. His occasional reprimands never showed temperament, but they were backed by a level of self-confidence that he had not possessed when he arrived in New Haven as a newly ordained priest. Six years of serving his parish and his faith at the same time had allowed him a rare degree of self-realization.

By nature, Father McGivney was disarmingly kindhearted and that was the side of his persona that St. Mary's parish found so appealing from the first and that made him so popular there. Meanwhile, he had also learned a lesson just as important for a priest, or for any clergyman: he had learned that to be *unpopular* when occasion demanded was crucial as well. In that sense, McGivney was especially fortunate to be working in the pastorate of Father Lawlor, who seemed to operate under the belief that loyalty was something to be bestowed, rather than expected. Lawlor was a steady source of support in McGivney's myriad activities as well as his occasional contretemps.

The founding of the Knights of Columbus had been a part of the tempering of Michael McGivney's personality. The first year had certainly been rocky, with clashes that gave him no choice but to fight for what he held to be true about the group. During the tense times, there was nowhere for him to hide, if he wanted the brand-new group to succeed, and no one to fight his battles for him. In Driscoll, Mullen, Geary, Sellwood, and the others, he had good friends, but at the same time they were aggressive businessmen and tough adversaries. McGivney could not have seen his own idea for the order prevail with such men if he hadn't developed a thick hide and the ability to win a point in a fair fight, or even the occasional unfair one.

The same week that the *Union* reporter dropped by to interview Fathers McGivney and Lawlor, the Knights of Columbus held their first annual convention in New Haven. By that time, there were five councils and 459 members. Meriden was leading the way, with two councils and 219 Knights, but the New Haven founders still dominated the Supreme Council. James Mullen presided as Supreme Knight.[20]

Councils were sprouting like bulbs in the spring. "The Knights of Columbus are prospering finely," commented the *New Haven Morning Journal and Courier,* though the word might just as well have been "finally." Towns outside of Connecticut were sending inquiries and the Supreme Council was arranging charters to accommodate them. For all of the satisfaction Father McGivney took in the spreading of his ideals, encompassed in the motto of the order—"Unity, Charity"— the Knights seemed to be outgrowing his ability to serve as an officer. Despite the suspicions of some people within the diocese, McGivney had never sought to establish a power base for himself with the Knights. In 1884, with the order flourishing and the opportunity for immense influence lying well within his grasp, Father McGivney declined to allow himself to be reelected as secretary of the Supreme Council. That June, he told Mullen to tell the others that he would be too busy with his sacred duties thenceforth to continue his administrative role in the Knights. He would, however, continue as chaplain.

Michael McGivney was letting go of the organization and leaving it to the organization itself, which he had specifically designed to outlive any one person. Although it would have been very easy to do, he did not create the Knights as a monument to his own irreplaceability. He created it to continue in perpetuity, and as far as he was concerned, the sooner it stood on its own, the better for all. In fact, it took far greater strength for McGivney to let the group go than it would have to hold on and cultivate it around the force of his own personality. Whether or not he had been under any pressure within the diocese to surrender direct influence over the order, he was comfortable in being, once again, nothing more or less than a parish priest.

On November 2, Father McGivney's greatest concern was the national election that was to be held two days later. In the bitter contest for the presidency, Grover Cleveland was running against James Blaine, a former senator who lost a large measure of the Roman Catholic vote when one of his supporters made a speech alluding to the close relationship of "rum, Romanism and rebellion." Despite the widespread disturbance over that unfortunately catchy phrase, Michael McGivney didn't take any sides. The only admonishment he issued did indicate, however, the kind of election that it was— during Sunday services, he advised his parishioners not to sell their votes.[21]

After the services, Cleveland supporters were standing

outside St. Mary's Church handing out flyers, repeating the "rum, Romanism and rebellion" outrage. They were soon joined by Blaine men, handing out circulars downplaying the remark. A Cleveland supporter, said to be attending services at St. Mary's for the first time in years, ran up the steps and into the church. He sought out Father McGivney and accosted him, shouting, "If you don't rebuke this thing, I pity you!"[22] Other members of the congregation rushed to the overexcited politician, horrified that anyone would speak to a priest in such a way. McGivney, for his part, saw nothing to rebuke. He would not, as he had made clear in his comments, take sides in the election.

Father McGivney, along with everyone else in the country, spent the following Wednesday waiting for the election results to be tabulated (Cleveland would not be declared the winner until Saturday). In the afternoon, however, he received a letter that made all else seem suddenly irrelevant. The letter was from the chancery in Hartford. It said that he was leaving St. Mary's.

The bishop was transferring Father McGivney to the town of Thomaston, where the Catholic church had been without a pastor since the death of Father Gaffney the previous summer. McGivney was due to start there in eight days. Clearly, he was ready for his own pastorate. Thomaston, however, did represent something of a backwater compared with New Haven. Nevertheless, his place was not to question the wisdom of the decision or the relative status of Thomaston as a parish. He was a parish priest and any church was an opportunity to serve.

At his last Sunday Mass as curate of St. Mary's, Father

McGivney said his farewell, concluding, "I have been with you for seven long years, visiting your sick and guiding the steps of your children in the paths in which they should go. At times I have been harsh to some of you, but it was only when I thought it for your good. If by any action of mine I have given scandal or offense to the least among you, then I pray you to forgive me. Wherever I go, the memory of the people of St. Mary's and their great kindness to me will always be uppermost in my heart. Once again my friends, good-bye."

The mood at St. Mary's was captured in an article published in the *New Haven Evening Register* and probably written by John J. Splain:

> Never, it seemed, was a congregation so affected by the parting address of a clergyman as the great audience which filled St. Mary's yesterday. Some of those present wept aloud and others sobbed audibly. Scarcely one among them has not been the recipient of some kind act or favor from Father McGivney, and his great popularity was clearly shown by the remarks which the people passed as they filed out of church.
>
> There was never a more energetic or hard working young priest stationed in New Haven than he.[23]

14

TALK OF THE TOWN

As parents and disciplinarians, Dr. and Mrs. Edwin Harwood had a singular reflex—and quite a delightful one for a certain kind of child. Whenever one of their offspring veered from the path of acceptable behavior, the Harwoods stopped everything and went away. Rebellious Harwoods weren't confined to their rooms; quite the opposite. They got to go to resorts all over New England. If the offense was particularly galling, they were swept off to Europe.

All of that may explain why James Harwood ended up in self-exile in Montana. He probably figured that it saved time.

In 1884, when Alida was caught in the act of commuting to New York City in order to take formal instruction in the Roman Catholic faith, she was sentenced to a summer on Mount Desert Island in Maine. Mount Desert Island was a universe of natural beauty, first-class accommodations, socialites by the score, and not one Catholic church. Honora Harwood accompanied her big sister, who confided en route that she not only wanted to become a Catholic but perhaps even a nun.

Honora was not inclined in the same direction, attracting as she did an embarrassment of suitors on Mount Desert Island. At varying times in the day, the place seemed to swarm with blackflies and eligible Ivy Leaguers. A girl like Honora needed netting. After a serious flirtation with a Harvard man named Truman Hemingway, who had an income but not yet his full inheritance, Honora accepted a marriage proposal from John V. L. Pruyn, scion of one of the old Dutch families along the Hudson River. He already had his inheritance. Pruyn was a perfect gentleman, except for one thing: he had already proposed to a girl back in Albany, who waffled a bit and then, with sorely inconvenient timing, accepted him right after Honora did.

None of that was Honora's fault, exactly, but it did set the backdrop for a Harwood trip to England in the summer of 1885. Alida had also earned a place on the excursion. She had by then been baptized by a Jesuit priest at St. John's College in New York. With Father McGivney having left St. Mary's, she attended New Haven's German Catholic church, mostly because it did not receive as much press attention as St. Mary's; no Catholic church in town did. She didn't want to generate any publicity that might embarrass her father. Alida's parents stoically accepted her conversion, but when Dr. Harwood learned that her next plan was to enter a convent, he lowered the boom. He "sent her to Europe to rid herself of the notion."[1]

Alida and Honora sailed off in the company of Mrs. Harwood.

In midsummer, something finally went right for the Reverend Edwin Harwood where his errant daughters were concerned. In a gesture worthy of any romantic novel, John Pruyn hopped on a ship to England, sought out Honora, and begged her to forgive him his past blundering. Somewhere in the course of the conversation he convinced her that he was entirely free of his former love in Albany. In the end, Honora agreed to be his wife.

Not even Honora—not even John Pruyn—could have been as pleased about the engagement as was Dr. Harwood. Unable to contain himself, he booked passage on a transatlantic liner so that he could join his family, including his future son-in-law. With Alida assuring him in London that she had given up the idea of becoming a nun, the outlook was brighter for the old minister than it had been since his children had been too young to think for themselves—and that was a long time since. The wedding was set for October 7, at Trinity Church in New Haven, of course. Alida would be maid of honor. Dr. Harwood would perform the ceremony and then see the newlyweds off on their honeymoon (to Colorado). And then, just four days later, he would preside over the opening of the Protestant Episcopal Church Congress in his hometown.

By the middle of 1885, Father McGivney had settled into the rather less swirling mode of life in Thomaston. When twelve new men in one week were hired in the clock factories there, it overshadowed all other news. Socially, the town was fixated on its roller-skating rink, which managed to engage the world's champion female roller skater for an exhibition. That was news, too.

As soon as Father McGivney was comfortable in his role as pastor of St. Thomas's Church, he began to display his own social sense, taking an interest in the Christian Doctrine Society. The members, numbering about one hundred, raised money to stock a parish library and give awards for excellence in Sunday school.[2] The revenues were drawn largely from plays presented on St. Patrick's Day. That was an exercise with which McGivney was familiar, and in time he was asked to direct a production of *Eileen Oge,* one of the hits of his days with the St. Joseph's TAL in New Haven.

With councils of the Knights of Columbus forming at the rate of about one every other week in 1885, the *Connecticut Catholic* began to devote a column in nearly every issue to its activities. In one accompanying editorial, John Scanlon, the editor, amiably referred to the K. of C. as "a secret society." That elicited a rather vinegary letter from a priest who signed himself only as "Clericus." It read in part:

> The question of secret societies is at present a paramount one among Catholics; and it is needless to say that no secret society, properly so called, can exist in the Church. Your assertion, therefore, that the Knights of Columbus is to be classed among secret societies has caused no little surprise among your readers. I respectfully request you, then, to state in

your next issue in what this secrecy consists, why
there should be secrecy in such an organization, and
if, in proclaiming the society to be a secret one, you
are not going beyond the intention of its founder.

Justice to the young men of the diocese requires
you to give an answer to those questions.[3]

The letter touched a sore point with Father McGivney.
For three years, he had been as sensitive as a master diplomat
to whisperings against the new organization. He had maneu-
vered the group around all those issues and personalities that
held the potential to ruin it. In the late spring of 1885, however, with the Knights of Columbus having shown its worth
in the formation of twenty-two councils, and in the very real
support of four bereaved families, McGivney was impatient
with anyone who would bring criticism of the group to a
public forum before first consulting the "founder." He took
Clericus's letter as a gratuitous attack on the Knights of
Columbus and composed a reply.

In the meantime, Scanlon took his best shot at an answer for
Clericus. He attempted to respond on theological grounds, even
while admitting that his knowledge in that realm did not match
that of his inquisitor. Scanlon's editorial quoted at length edicts
on the subject of secret societies issued by the Third Plenary
Council of Baltimore, a convocation of the American Catholic
leadership for the interpretation of church law in the United
States. The First Plenary Council had been held in 1852 and the
second in 1866. The decrees of the Third, held in late 1884,
were still very fresh on the minds of Catholics that spring.[4]

The Second Plenary Council had long since forbidden

Catholics to belong to secret societies, and in fact it was part of the backdrop that influenced Father McGivney to found the Knights of Columbus. In a sense, it put the onus on parish priests like McGivney, by forcing them to withhold absolution from any person who belonged to a secret organization. Specifically, the Second Plenary Council reiterated the Vatican's condemnation of the Masons, but neither it nor the Third Plenary Council cited any other groups by name. The designation of offending organizations was left to individual bishops, who were expected to conduct investigations of potentially offensive societies operating within their dioceses.[5]

John Scanlon's editorial in the *Connecticut Catholic* quoted the pastoral letter that was composed in English from the Plenary Council's decrees (which were issued in Latin): "If any society's obligation be such as to bind its members to secrecy, even when rightly questioned by competent authority, then such a society puts itself outside the limits of approval, and no one can be a member of it and at the same time be admitted to the Sacraments of the Catholic Church." Scanlon allowed that the Knights of Columbus was a secret society, but quickly pointed out that in essence, it was a business institution and so, like all businesses and especially insurance ones, it had to have its secrets. Furthermore, he added his own interpretation of canon law. "Any organization, as we understand, gotten up for a good purpose," he wrote, "and proposing to attain the end in view by legitimate, moral and legal ends, will meet with the approval of the Church. The mere fact of secrecy does not bring condemnation to any society."[6]

And so John Scanlon and the *Connecticut Catholic* had come to Father McGivney's defense. McGivney appreciated the gesture, but he didn't want help. As a matter of fact, the editorial seemed to irk McGivney almost as much as Clericus's original letter. One can almost see him sitting at his desk in the rectory in Thomaston and dashing off his reply, with perhaps a bit too much haste, but with a great deal of satisfaction in finally telling off a detractor of his beloved Knights of Columbus:

Editor *Connecticut Catholic:*

I had occasion lately to read one of your latest editorials headed: "Secret Societies—Knights of Columbus" and preambled by a query from a certain "Clericus" who seems anxious to add to his store of theology by applying to you, although you graciously admit that he knows more of the sacred science than you. Had Clericus applied to the proper source for information he would not have been the cause of such widespread misrepresentation with regard to the Knights of Columbus.

Since the article in question seems to reflect upon the "founder" as belonging to a secret society and since he (the founder) is supposed to have known what he intended when he organized the Knights of Columbus, I deem it but "justice to the young men of the diocese" to permit "the founder" to make known his intentions. "The Order of the Knights of Columbus is the same now as when first instituted," viz: It is an Order composed of Catholics and instituted for the welfare of Catholic families in the State of Connecticut. It has no connection whatever with the Church, except that Catholic priests are among its members and Catholic priests, whether members or not, can attend any of the meetings.

From the fact that the Order has been formed upon purely business principles, it has not asked for, nor did it need, the approbation of the authorities of the diocese any more than an insurance company composed of Catholics would ask the Rt. Rev. Bishop to approve its by-laws and constitution.

The authorities of the Church are only too anxious to foster any society which will better the conditions of her children provided that the by-laws and constitution do not conflict with the rules and regulations of the Church.

The constitution and by-laws of the Knights of Columbus contain nothing collusive to the rules of the Church. Although but a few years organized, the Order has effected incalculable good in many households. Not only in sickness, but when death takes the support of the family away, the Knights of Columbus comes to the relief of the widow and the orphan in a very substantial manner.

Had there been anything objectionable in the business of the different councils, I would be most likely to have seen it in my connection with the order since its foundation. You will please, therefore, correct two misstatements in a recent issue, and say in your journal that the order of the Knights of Columbus is not a secret society, and that it has not been approved by the Rt. Rev. Bishop. By doing so you will remove the "surprise" from the minds of your readers, and thereby confer a favor upon "the young men of the diocese" by enlightening "Clericus."

> I remain
> Yours Truly
> M. J. McGivney
> FOUNDER OF THE KNIGHTS OF COLUMBUS[7]

Clericus responded by sending one last note to the paper, accusing Father McGivney of overreacting. Perhaps he did, but his letter was much more than just a swipe at Clericus. In the first place, it was a swift denunciation of any attempt to separate him, as founder, from the Knights of Columbus. More important, it was a reinterpretation of the order in light of the Third Plenary Council's decrees.

By denying that the bishop had approved the Knights, McGivney seems at first to be forgetting that he himself had once proudly publicized that the Knights of Columbus was formed "by permission of our Rt. Rev. Bishop."[8] According to the processes outlined by the Third Plenary Council, however, Bishop McMahon's permissions were only unofficial ones; he had never formally conducted an investigation of the Knights of Columbus.

Nor would the bishop have reason to investigate: the order was not a secret society, according to Father McGivney's 1885 letter. While it did have rites unknown to the prying public, any priest was allowed to attend any meeting. That was the open window that kept the Knights of Columbus from being a secret society.

McGivney, in his letter, described the special relationship that the Knights of Columbus would have with the Catholic Church. He was no longer talking in theory, but out of actual practice. The Church would be to the Knights of Columbus as an accounting firm is to a business. There was no direct connection and no authority from on high, yet for its own good, the Knights allowed the Church, in the form of its priests, the freedom to audit any and every aspect of the order's activities, but with a particular focus on the spiritual and moral ones.

Although a great deal had happened since Michael McGivney founded the Knights of Columbus, he continued to see the group more clearly than anyone else. Even while he devoted himself to his parish in Thomaston, he kept a wary eye out for any attempt to undermine the Knights. He was right if he thought of himself as its best defender. In August, he agreed to participate in the order's first parade, a bold public debut that took several thousand Knights, in regalia, through the streets of New Haven. Riding in a carriage amid the many marchers, Father McGivney took care to invite one of his fellow chaplains along. He never wanted to be singled out, certainly not in an organization founded as a brotherhood. After the parade, he made a presentation to James Mullen on behalf of the rest of the Supreme Council, giving him a fancy pocket watch in recognition of his work in expanding the order.

As the summer of 1885 ended, the Harwood family returned to America in something like triumph, looking forward to all that October promised to bring. There was a great deal to do. Honora, for her part, was particularly busy, accepting one present after another from her fiancé, including diamonds in various settings and "a quantity of rare old lace which had been worn by the mother of the groom at her wedding." That was to be used in the dress. With so many people in the city looking forward to the wedding as "the social event of the year," the Harwoods had to go over their lists with meticulous care. It wasn't easy to decide on whom to bestow an invitation—just which members of New Haven's rich old families and exactly how many Trowbridges, Hillhouses, and Ingersolls.

Sometime after arriving in New Haven, though, the family had a more sobering worry. Alida contracted malaria, then a common disease during hot, humid summers, even in New England. The conditions happened to be especially ripe that year. Alida's case was not serious, however, and since she was a strong young woman of twenty-five, the doctors were not concerned about her recovery. She rested much of the day but was still available to help her sister prepare for the wedding. At the very least, the two could talk endlessly about it as the October 7 date approached.

In the last week of September, invitations went out to 150 guests. The *New Haven Evening Register* said that it was going to be "a very brilliant affair," and the *Morning News* commented that "society was on tip toe of expectation."[9]

On Monday, September 28, Honora and a friend went into New York City for a day or two of shopping. Sometime Tuesday evening, she sent a letter to her parents, informing them that she had met Truman Hemingway, her beau from Mount Desert Island, while in New York and had, in fact, married him. She thoughtfully enclosed a copy of the marriage certificate, along with her hope that they would pardon her for changing her mind. She closed by noting that by the time they received the letter, on Wednesday morning, she and Truman would already be on the high seas, sailing for Germany on board a liner called the *Werra*.

The elopement was greeted as a spectacular development in both New Haven and New York. Both cities ignited with gossip. Only one corner of New Haven stayed dark. Reporters who staked out the Harwood household couldn't detect a thing. The windows were drawn and nearly every light was out. No one came in the house or went out. A person who considered himself a friend of the family predicted that Dr. Harwood would never fully recover from the shock.

And that was before Harwood saw the front page of Thursday's *Evening Register*. Right next to a bulging piece on "The Harwood Sensation" was a depressingly chipper column on all the bright plans in place for the Protestant Episcopal Church Congress, which was only a few weeks away.

Mrs. Harwood, no less than her husband, was heartsick at the news. As for Alida, she had taken just enough of a turn for the worse while her sister was in New York that she was entirely bedridden. The family was afraid to tell her of the elopement. They were right. When she was finally told, the emotional upset proved too much for her. The fever took hold and only grew stronger with the passing days. Two weeks later, the best doctors in the city conferred on the case and advised Dr. and Mrs. Harwood that there was no hope for Alida's recovery.[10]

By October 14, Alida Harwood was unconscious nearly all

of the time. When she was able to talk, she asked for Father Michael McGivney, "her favorite advisor and friend in the matter of her religion," according to a person who was present.[11] Her parents demurred. Even in delirium, however, Alida was insistent. The last wish that she expressed was that Father McGivney come. She wanted him to perform the rites that even she knew she must need. At almost four o'clock on the fifteenth, Alida died.

Two days later, Honora and Truman landed in Bremen. Episcopal churchmen from all over the United States were leaving their homes, bound for the congress in New Haven. During the span of those two days, very little had happened inside the Trinity rectory. Alida's body had been laid out, cloaked all in white. Yet there were no firm plans for a funeral. Dr. Harwood was practically unreachable. When he did agree to speak, he was still against calling for a Catholic priest, McGivney or any other. Mrs. Harwood understood that he did not want his daughter taken from him in any form, not from his home and not from the religion to which he had devoted his life. But Father McGivney's presence had been Alida's last wish.

Honora no sooner disembarked from the *Werra* than she and her husband were back on the seas again, rushing home from Germany after receiving a telegram about her sister's death. By that point, there weren't many people in New Haven and New York who weren't tired of the thought of Honora Harwood Hemingway. Somehow, she was no longer quite so attractive—just a former belle who had broken three hearts too many.

Mrs. Harwood proved unable to ignore the echo of her

daughter's final words. On October 18, she made a decision. She sent a letter to Thomaston, requesting that Father Mc-Givney please come to her family. He did so immediately.

With that, more rumors ran the gossip circuit in New Haven, as the sight of Reverend Father McGivney alighting from a carriage and walking up the steps to the Trinity rectory confirmed that Alida Harwood had indeed died as a Catholic. "There had been rumors to that effect for some time," observed a paper, "but there were many of her friends who did not believe that the daughter of the first Episcopal churchman in Connecticut had been a convert."[12]

Father McGivney, grief-stricken himself, found the Harwoods in a wretched state, in a daze of pain that just barely allowed them to function. Families in trouble always elicited his most loving sympathy and Mr. and Mrs. Harwood, whatever their religion, were no exception. Nothing was certain when he met them for the first time. He wasn't at all sure that he would be permitted to view the body. He didn't even know exactly why he had been called, until he saw their helpless faces.

With Michael McGivney's help, the Harwoods finally planned a funeral for their daughter. The priest surprised them by offering no objection to their holding an Episcopal service for her. McGivney had never heard of a dual ceremony—one according to Catholic rites and one according to Episcopal ones—but he could see that it would help Dr. Harwood immeasurably. He assured his Protestant colleague that there was no reason from a Catholic point of view that it had to be one or the other. Inwardly, he knew that as long as Catholic prayers were read and absolution given, it didn't make any difference what happened afterward.[13]

The next day, Father McGivney returned to the Episcopal rectory. Alida's body lay in a casket in the bedroom where she had once slept. A solid silver cross, provided by her parents, sat on top of the coffin. With the drapes drawn, the room was nearly dark. About a dozen people were in the room. According to a witness, McGivney "attired in his cossack [*sic*], surplice and stole, with the flicker of a blessed candle illuminating his countenance, presented a picture long to be remembered, as with a voice that almost trembled with the grief he felt for the dead he read the mournful Latin prayers for the repose of the soul of the fair creature in the casket before him."[14] When Father McGivney was finished, six pallbearers took the casket to Trinity Church. Several of the pallbearers were young men who had been planning to serve as ushers in Honora's wedding. Another was John Pruyn, Honora's former fiancé, who had come from Albany for the funeral. Just before four o'clock, the Episcopal service ended, and the Trinity Church bell tolled its own requiem.

That evening, the Protestant Episcopal Church Congress opened with an overflow of delegates, but without its founder. "Rev. Dr. Harwood will be unable to attend," explained an article covering the celebratory atmosphere of the congress, "as he will go to Hempstead, L.I. tonight with the remains of his daughter."[15]

At least Dr. Harwood had finally left his study behind, along with some part of his despair. Father McGivney, arriving when the famed minister was himself in need of kind words of counsel, offered a kind of proof that Alida hadn't left Harwood's family when she became a Catholic. Dr. Harwood didn't need to think of Alida as parted from him, except temporarily. She was still his girl—nothing changed that.

15

A PRIEST'S LIFE

Long into the night of December 16, 1885, the air was quiet around St. Thomas's Church, sitting by itself on a rise near the center of Thomaston. The stillness was unbroken by anyone or anything. St. Thomas's was a thickset building in dark brownstone, with a square tower sprouting out of the left-hand corner in the front. It had been built by the late Father Eugene Gaffney, who apparently set more value on a solid building than a graceful one. Father Gaffney had also overseen construction of the rectory on the lot next door to the church.

That night, all was not still inside the rectory. Two burglars made quick work of breaking into the ground floor of the house. They didn't touch anything but made their way immediately to Father McGivney's safe. Their scheme wasn't quite as brazen as stealing from the collection plate on a Sunday, but it was the next best thing. Or the next worst. Oblivious of the scene downstairs, McGivney was asleep in his room. Other members of the rectory staff were also in bed for the night. Meanwhile, the burglars were going about their work, drilling holes in the thick iron door of the safe. They knew just where to drill in order to free the door. In the days before power tools, it was hard work, but at least a hand drill didn't make much noise. The slumbering people upstairs never would have heard it.

The rectory dog was a much lighter sleeper. Even shut into the cellar for the night, he barked up a storm when he heard the burglars. By the time Michael McGivney came downstairs to investigate, the thieves had disappeared. Although the safecrackers were never caught, McGivney had his suspicions as to where they were from.[1] In the first place, they probably weren't from Thomaston.

Thomaston was a clock town. It was named after Seth Thomas, the most famous clockmaker in the country, and it was, by no coincidence, home to his thriving company. His son expanded the firm and along the way also donated the land on which St. Thomas's Church was built. The safecrackers might have been from Thomaston, but it is more likely that they came from nearby Terryville.

Terryville was a lock town, home of the gigantic Eagle Lock Company—which also made safes. If Father McGivney harbored suspicions, they probably had something to do with Terryville. Regardless, the case of the rectory burglars was never solved.

Between clock making and locksmithing, the twin towns

of Thomaston and Terryville depended heavily on factory workers and they each drew on immigrant labor of the type that was responsible for the staggering expansion of the Catholic Church in the United States in the late nineteenth century.

As Father McGivney soon realized, Thomaston parish was very different from his former home at St. Mary's, back in New Haven. The people were more uniformly working class, which meant, at least in the booming 1880s, that there were fewer who were destitute than in a big city such as New Haven. On the other hand, the parish also lacked that band of educated and ambitious sophisticates who had circled around McGivney at St. Mary's.

Michael McGivney brought the same manner to all human souls. Nonetheless, he must have missed the stimulating conversations he had in New Haven with the likes of Edward Downes, Stephen Maher, and Cornelius Driscoll. In Thomaston, he found a good friend in Tim Burns, a grocer, and he was also close to the sprawling Mack family—they were the ones who owned the skating rink. But whatever it was that he missed in the rare blend of friends he had in New Haven was more than replaced by Thomaston's close proximity to Waterbury, ten miles away.

Father McGivney found time for frequent visits to see his mother and his sister Annie, who was studying to become a schoolteacher. At their home on Railroad Hill Street, he was just Michael, as always. McGivney's two young brothers, John and Patrick, were in school and pleased him no end by expressing sincere interest in following him into the priesthood. Occasionally, Father McGivney delivered the sermon in services at his boyhood church, Immaculate Conception in Waterbury, renewing even more of his old ties and friendships. After more than a dozen years away, he probably regarded them as more valuable than ever.

In March 1886, Father McGivney received news of the type that was tragically familiar in his life in the Church: another friend in the priesthood was dead. It was Father Lawlor, who was also his brother-in-law. As pastor of St. Mary's in New Haven, Patrick Lawlor had been consistently encouraging to McGivney. At only forty-five and after four years of illness, Father Lawlor finally succumbed to what was described as "brain congestion." Most parishioners and even some printed obituaries attributed the death more specifically to worry over St. Mary's debt.[2] Michael McGivney attended the funeral and the sight of him back in New Haven made many people predict that he would soon return him to his former church, in the role of pastor. But that was not to be.

Perhaps the bishop just didn't have the heart to ask another priest to take over St. Mary's. It seemed to be tantamount to a death sentence. As the diocese was well aware in the 1880s, parish priests did not generally live very long, under any circumstances. From 1874 to 1886, the Hartford Diocese counted about eighty-three priests at any one time. Yet during that same span, seventy diocesan priests died.[3] That translates to a turnover of almost 85 percent in a dozen years. Going into the priesthood, young men knew that they had little chance of reaching fifty years of age and almost no hope of reaching seventy. One reason was exposure to disease, but Protestant ministers presumably made the same sorts of calls on the ill and destitute. Plenty of ministers lived to celebrate their silver jubilees in Connecticut in the late nineteenth century.[4]

The plain fact is that priests were trapped in a vicious circle. They were overworked because there were not enough priests to serve a Catholic population that had long since grown past 150,000 in the state of Connecticut. The short life span of the average priest led to even more work for those who were left—and that started the cycle all over again.

So it was that in 1886 Father McGivney did not receive the assignment to return to St. Mary's. The bishop couldn't spare him, or anyone else, to the buzz saw of St. Mary's debt. Instead, he arranged to turn St. Mary's Church over to an outside group, the Order of Preachers, better known as the Dominicans. Backed by the resources of an international religious organization, the new pastor of St. Mary's, Father Arthur V. Higgins, could face the church debt with something like new hope.

At almost the same time, the priest in charge of the Roman Catholic church in Terryville was reassigned and his parish was made adjunct to St. Thomas's Church. And so, the ongoing shortage of priests affected Father McGivney directly, as his workload immediately doubled. The two towns are barely three miles apart as the crow flies, but a priest in a horse-drawn carriage didn't have it quite as easy as that, facing hilly roads that were rugged in the best of weather. On Sunday mornings, Father McGivney celebrated Mass in Thomaston at 8:00 A.M., drove his carriage to Terryville for the 9:30 service, and then returned to Thomaston for an 11:00 service.[5] On clear summer mornings, it probably wasn't too much of a strain.

Father McGivney's responsibilities were prodigious, even without the addition of Terryville. In addition to all of his sacred duties, he was directing the Christian Doctrine Society in a production of *Handy Andy,* at the Thomaston Opera House. The highlight was said to have come when J. J. Mack, who managed the roller-skating rink by day, twisted his knee just walking across the stage.[6] He must have been nervous. At any rate, it stopped the show until everyone in the cast and in the audience could see that he was all right and then comment on the fact that he could skate on wheels all day, but just walking across a stage, he mangled himself.

McGivney was also resuscitating the Holy Name Society at St. Thomas's, running the semiannual church fairs, creating new excitement for the students in Sunday school, and acting as chaplain of the local Knights of Columbus council. He may also have been acting as third-base coach, since the council was in the process of forming a baseball team.[7] It is not hard to think who might have been behind that idea.

The parishioners were a bit bowled over by Michael McGivney's sheer energy. Someone termed him "zealous," which was one way to put it.[8] Another was that he loved his parishioners. The only thing he liked better than working with them on grand plans and projects was standing back and watching them work together, under the light of Christ.

Father McGivney was certainly an impresario, if only in that he was a man who made things happen. In the narrower sense of the word, he was a natural-born director, with a steady stream of newspaper reviews noting that time and again the performers in his shows surpassed all limitations.

Father McGivney was undoubtedly sensitive to music and

its power to inspire—or to irritate. In the case of the choir at St. Thomas's Church, he was suffering the latter sensation. Two years after he arrived, he had his own inspiration, inviting his sister Annie to play the organ at St. Thomas's and direct the singers. "Our choir is greatly improving under the management of Miss Annie McGivney," reported a parishioner in April 1886.[9]

For five weeks that fall, Father McGivney was busy directing his own group: the children of the Sunday school, who were preparing for a Thanksgiving production. It was no mere afternoon recital, but a full-blown extravaganza at the Opera House. About a week before the show, McGivney was driving his carriage into Waterbury when his horse panicked for some reason. The animal bolted with such force that Father McGivney could only struggle in vain to slow him down. Instead, the poor horse collided with an iron fence and died. The carriage tumbled after him and was wrecked but, fortunately, McGivney jumped clear and saved himself from injury.[10] He didn't even miss a rehearsal.

On the night before Thanksgiving, a huge audience was seated at the Opera House to see what the show was all about. Not all of the people in attendance had relatives in the cast, and that is saying something when it comes to a Sunday school production. As act after act went by, a little mug named Joe Conway had the crowd roaring with laughter, playing Medicine Jack. James Morris made them cry and "brought down the house," by singing a ballad called "Mother and I." Michael McGivney, it seems, had the audience in the palm of his hand—but only because he had his players feeling so good about themselves.

"He has been the best friend to the youth since he came here," marveled a parishioner at St. Thomas's, speaking of Father McGivney.[11] Aside from the organized activities, Mc-Givney was available to the young people for serious counseling on their religion or for casual conversation about practically anything. In any situation, grave or jovial, he represented the same firm beliefs. Children and teens trying to sort things in their own lives came to depend on him, if no one else.

In 1887, Father McGivney had the rare satisfaction of announcing to his congregation that the Thomaston parish no longer had so much as "one cent of debt."[12] During the following year, he was in a position to install a few of the modern wonders of his day at the rectory. First, there was electricity, which was a convenience for him. Next there was a telephone, which was a convenience for his parishioners. It must have seemed a mixed blessing to him at times.

"If Father McGivney could be said to have ever had one single worldly ambition," commented Father Joseph Daley, "it was to hope that his brothers might enjoy a good education." When John McGivney graduated from Waterbury High School, he was the valedictorian of his class.[13]

The dearest wish of Michael McGivney's heart, again according to Father Daley, was that John and Patrick would someday become priests.[14] Both were on that path, attending a seminary near Boston, when Mary McGivney fell ill in 1888; they came rushing home to see her. Father McGivney was already at her bedside in the house on Railroad Hill Street. On December 8, she died. Her son Michael sang the solemn Requiem High Mass at her funeral.[15]

By 1888, the Knights of Columbus counted 4020 members in forty-three councils. Father McGivney had remained quietly involved, but he did not take an active position in the power struggles that roiled the fast-growing organization. Nor did he have much to say about the move, which was ultimately successful, to replace the Supreme Council with a more legislative Board of Government. The board was charged with electing the Supreme Knight, and in 1886 it chose a Bridgeport lawyer, John Phelan, to fill that post.

Father McGivney was more concerned that the order remain true to those themes with the greatest influence over the members and their families. The wife of a Knight in New London wrote a poem to express those themes. Despite the fact that the poet couldn't think of anything to rhyme with "Columbus" except "purpose," the poem was flattering in the way that it reiterated McGivney's goals and proved that they were still intact, whatever the feuding in the executive offices. Reprinted in several Connecticut newspapers, it ran in part:

> The widow and orphan are helped from their hand
> At the husband and father's demise.
> They are true to their faith, too, by which they will stand
> Till death knocks at each of their doors. . . . [16]

With the appointment of an assistant pastor in Thomaston parish, Father McGivney had enough free time in 1888 to involve himself in the most significant development within the Knights of Columbus since the order was founded six years before. A group of Catholic men in Providence, Rhode Island, requested permission to form a council—the first one outside of the state of Connecticut.

On July 8, the Tyler Council was initiated in Providence. According to one of the early officers (a man who signed his account "Tempus"), the ceremony was very exciting. Practically nothing happened in the ensuing six months, however. Potential members were awaiting encouragement from the priests, who were awaiting encouragement from the bishop, Matthew Harkins, who just didn't seem much interested in the Knights of Columbus. On that note, everything stalled in Providence.

At the request of Supreme Knight Phelan, Father Mc-Givney traveled to Rhode Island in January 1889. His very first appointment was with the bishop of Providence. As Tempus explained, "The reverend chaplain of the order visited Providence and laid the object of the order and the good work that it is accomplishing before the Rt. Rev. Bishop Harkins, with the result of our receiving his approbation, and naturally that of his priests.

"Father McGivney," Tempus continued, "then advised the holding of a public meeting, with the result that on Tuesday evening, January 22, the hall of Tyler council was filled to overflowing with interested friends."[17] McGivney returned to Providence and spoke at the meeting, which was the true launch of both the Tyler Council and the growth of the Knights of Columbus across state borders and, ultimately, national ones as well.

The trips to Providence were Michael McGivney's last major effort on behalf of the Knights of Columbus. In 1889, the year he turned thirty-seven, his strength began to wane.

That peculiar malady, that certain strain of exhaustion that caught up to every priest in the nineteenth century, finally had the better of Michael McGivney. It left him vulnerable to any illness circulating among the people he served in Thomaston. That year, he was often sick with a cold, but he kept to his duties at St. Thomas's and at the church in Terryville, even overseeing one of his popular church fairs in the last week of November. In December, Father McGivney contracted influenza. In January 1890, it resulted in pneumonia.

While McGivney was confined to his bed, the flu epidemic was spreading throughout the country. Father McGivney survived the flu and recovered from his bout with pneumonia, but he was left with a weakness he could not overcome. In hopes of reclaiming his natural energy, he took a trip to Virginia in March. Thomaston parish was left in the hands of his assistant. It was irony without any bite—a wan reminder of the days in New Haven when Father Murphy traveled to resorts in search of his old verve, leaving St. Mary's to the wunderkind, Father Michael McGivney.

On returning from Virginia, Father McGivney spent two weeks in New Haven, under the care of Dr. Bacon, the physician who had accompanied him to Father Carmody's bedside seven years earlier. However, Dr. Bacon could do very little. Apparently, the flu had left McGivney with permanent damage to his system. Emaciated and pale, he went to New York City and consulted with specialists in internal medicine.[18] He wanted his health back; his parishioners needed him. He took another trip to the South, returning in June. The following month, he was confined to his bed in Thomaston, no longer able to rise. He retained his mental powers and, in a hoarse whisper, continually asked about various members of his parish. Aware that he was dying, he was at peace. During the last illness of his cherished friend Mary Ann Gaffney Sellwood nine years before, he had been impressed by her composure, deep in the embrace of Christ, as death approached. He often told her at the time that he only wished that he would be as well prepared to meet God as she was. In that slowing August of 1890, he was. It seems that in helping hundreds of other Catholics along the same course, he had also found the way himself. The only regret that he expressed was that he wouldn't be present at the ordination of his two younger brothers.

Father Michael McGivney died on the morning of August 14, 1890, two days after his thirty-eighth birthday. A solemn Requiem High Mass sent him to his place in eternity, but that still left the people on earth to try to remember him. There was a sermon, delivered by the pastor of St. Mary's in New Haven. There was a four-foot cross made of flowers and marked "Founder" and "Chaplain," the gift of the officers of the Knights of Columbus. There was the crowd at St. Thomas's, filling the church and spilling out to cover the entire lawn in the front.

Michael McGivney did something that few people have, especially in more modern times. He saw an opportunity, rising through it to prominence—and fame and power. Then, by his own choice and having already made his mark, he reverted to his original calling.

In the life of McGivney, there was that historical role which he filled masterfully, recognizing the pitfalls facing Catholic men in the urbanizing America of the nineteenth century. The fact that Father McGivney responded to what he saw by launching the Knights of Columbus gives him a permanent place at a critical juncture in social history. As important, though, is that other legacy of his life, as he felt called upon to live it. It is expressed quite simply in the fact that a parish priest is all that he wanted to be.

Being a priest changed McGivney, who had lived a fairly secluded life before his ordination. He became more activist than ever before, more extroverted in applying his natural optimism to actual plans and projects. He also became more assertive. He had no choice in that matter. Two aspects of McGivney's inner life never wavered, however, from his earliest days to his last. The first was his faith in Catholicism. For better or for worse, he did not question, he did not surmise. He believed—with impervious conviction. McGivney's second lifelong characteristic was an abiding empathy, with a spirit of kindness extraordinary in his time or any other. It was just that which made him as an apostle of Christ.

His life, however, was not described by great occasions or grand gestures. His was the humility of moments, and the power beheld in the lightest of touches. The epitaph that remembers Father McGivney best appeared in an unassuming article carried in a Waterbury newspaper a few years before he died. "We unintentionally omitted the name of the Rev. McGivney in yesterday's issue as one of the speakers at the opera house on Memorial Day," the paper noted. "Although his remarks were brief, they were enthusiastically received and the audience gave him a decided preference above the other speakers in the way of applause."[19] That was McGivney: with the lightest of touches, he never failed to reach forward. Such were his ways and for those who knew him, they were unforgettable.

EPILOGUE

"If any man serve me, let him follow me; and where I am, there shall also my servant be: if any man serve me, him will my Father honor."

—GOSPEL ACCORDING TO ST. JOHN, 12:26

At the time of Father Michael McGivney's death in 1890, the Knights of Columbus counted 6000 members.[1] During that year, with influenza on the rampage, death benefits were paid to sixty-six families.[2] One of the $1000 endowments went to Annie and Maggie McGivney, Michael's sisters. Maggie would later be married, as were each of her two older sisters. Annie McGivney remained single and became a well-known teacher in Waterbury.

According to Father McGivney's will, about one-half of his estate—valued in total at $5883.66—was left to his four sisters. He left his library and his engraved gold watch to his brother Patrick, who was nearly finished studying for the priesthood. He also directed that Patrick, as executor, use $2000 for the education of John McGivney, the youngest of the brothers. Finally, in a codicil added just days before he died, Michael directed that $500 be spent on a monument stone marking the burial places of himself and his "beloved parents."[3] Both John and Patrick McGivney were eventually ordained priests, fulfilling their older brother's wish. Each of the younger McGivneys would serve as Supreme Chaplain of the Knights of Columbus. So would one of Father McGivney's nephews. In fact, it would be the 1930s before someone outside of the McGivney clan served as Supreme Chaplain.

The Knights of Columbus did not forsake Michael McGivney or his role as founder, honoring him through the years in official publications and at gatherings. It was not merely the fact of McGivney's creation of the Knights that ensured that he could not be forgotten, but his spirit, which continued to permeate the order. In keeping with Father McGivney's original ideas, the group focused on individuals and their families. In 1922, when the organization celebrated its fortieth anniversary, the membership numbered 800,000.

Today, there are 1.7 million Knights of Columbus in the United States, Canada, the Philippines, Mexico, the Dominican Republic, Puerto Rico, Panama, the Bahamas, the Virgin Islands, Guatemala, Guam, and Saipan. Expansion into Poland is under way. The emphasis is still on helping men to care for their families, spiritually and in practical ways, too. The days when insurance payouts depended on special assessments have long since passed. As of 2004, the Knights had more than 1.5

million premium-based life insurance policies in effect. Annuities and long-term-care policies have been added to the traditional life insurance programs. The only aspect of the Knights of Columbus that has developed beyond that which Michael McGivney specifically envisioned is in charitable giving. In just one year, 2004, the local, state, and national councils made contributions totaling $135 million. The group is especially committed to scholarship grants and other educational causes, which would be consistent with McGivney's own priorities.

Father McGivney's role as the founder of the powerful Knights of Columbus may the basis of his fame today, but his most personal legacy lay in those lives he affected as a priest. Alfred Downes, the teenager for whom Father McGivney interceded in Probate Court in 1882, graduated from Yale Law School and later held the influential post of secretary to the mayor of New York City. Alfred married in the city and was the secretary of the Fire Department at the time of his death in 1907. He was the author of a book on the heroism of the horses he had come to know firsthand in the Fire Department.

Edward Downes Jr., Alfred's older brother, the seminarian who had to quit his studies in order to run the family's stationery store, also graduated from Yale Law School, as soon as the situation at home eased. Downes was a natural politician and was elected city clerk of New Haven in 1888. He remained close to Father McGivney and delivered a eulogy in his memory at a Knights of Columbus meeting in 1891. As he became recognized in national circles, Edward Downes was appointed as the State Department's consul general in Amsterdam.[4] When his term ended in 1897, however, he surprised many people by turning his back on politics and law in order to pursue his original dream of becoming a priest. Ordained in 1900, he served faithfully until his death in 1921.[5]

David Hillhouse Buel, who also followed Father McGivney into the priesthood, joined the Society of Jesuits. Father Buel became an educator, as do many Jesuits. He distinguished himself as the president of Georgetown University in Washington, D.C. Buel resigned from the Jesuit Society in 1912, however. Later that year, he was married and finished his life as an Episcopalian minister.[6]

Stephen Maher, the reporter who was one of Father McGivney's good friends, graduated from Yale Medical School in 1888. He devoted much of his career to the treatment of tuberculosis, isolating drugs effective in arresting various complications of the disease and overseeing the construction of five state sanitariums. In recognition of his efforts, Pope Pius XI created Dr. Maher a Knight of St. Gregory the Great in 1939.[7]

In 1997, Daniel A. Cronin, archbishop of the Hartford Diocese, initiated the process of canonization for Father Michael J. McGivney. With that, Father McGivney could be properly called a "servant of God," an appellation reserved for those being considered for sainthood. One of Bishop Cronin's first steps was appointing a postulator, Father Gabriel O'Donnell. The postulator is a combination of researcher and advocate who shepherds the cause through its many steps. For three years, Father O'Donnell searched for records pertaining to Father McGivney's life, an effort that resulted in a 700-page document called the *Acts*. In the year 2000, the *Acts* was formally presented to the Congregation for the Causes of Saints at the

Vatican. On the basis of the impression left by the *Acts,* the Congregation moved ahead with the appointment of a "relator," a member of the staff who evaluates the continuing process of canonization. The Congregation's chief relator, Father Ambrose Eszer, O.P., was appointed to Father McGivney's cause.

The Congregation for the Causes of Saints evaluates not only the *Acts* and related materials, but documentation of at least one miracle attributed to the intercession of Father Mc-Givney. A miracle is regarded as a sign from the Almighty that the person under consideration for sainthood has His approval. When the first miracle is accepted by the Congregation, a person can be beatified. He or she can thence be called a "blessed servant of God." When a second miracle is acknowledged, the canonization is complete and sainthood is conferred.

Father Michael McGivney would be the first American-born parish priest to be canonized. For the time being, Catholics around the world revere Father McGivney, including him in their prayers and contemplation. In that so many people still look to him for guidance, he will ever be in the relationship that suited him best: a parish priest for a modern world.

Acknowledgments

We are indebted to the libraries of LeMoyne College in Syracuse, New York, and Niagara University in Lewiston, New York, for use of their extensive collections on Roman Catholic history. The Connecticut State Historical Society, the Connecticut State Library, Yale University, Tulane University, the New Haven Free Library, the Connecticut French-Canadian Genealogical Society, and the New Haven Colony Historical Society were also important in the research. We are obliged to the John Paul II Cultural Center at the Catholic University of America in Washington, D.C., for guidance at key points in our work on the book.

Paul R. Keroack of Connecticut undertook a masterly research project some years ago on the Downes family of New Haven. As a private venture, he typed their story into manuscript form and left copies at several libraries. The authors are indebted to his work for shedding light on a family so important to the story of Michael McGivney. In addition, Paul was helpful with other suggestions during continuing research on our book.

Kathryn Cooke was helpful early on with research material on Meriden, Connecticut, and later reviewed the chapters for us. Kay has lived in Meriden all of her life, and we were fortunate to have her as a guide through its history.

Another friend in the effort behind this book was Susan Brosnan, archivist at the Knights of Columbus Supreme Council in New Haven. No one could have been more helpful in leading us through the collections of the K of C and advising us on the location of other materials. She deserves our deepest gratitude. The archives, it should be noted, are located at the Knights of Columbus Museum in New Haven. Among the items at the museum are many related to the life of Father McGivney, including his pocket watch, some of his clothing, and his date book. Mary Lou Cummings, the curator of the museum, went out of her way to help us to find many of the illustrations used in this book.

Father Gabriel O'Donnell, postulator of Father McGivney's cause for sainthood, has our sincere gratitude. Long a teacher in seminaries and at the college level, he was always available to us for discussions. Encouraging but never insistent, his was the spirit that made this project a continuing exploration of the type that serves to enthrall historians.

Lindy Boggs, former U. S. Ambassador to the Vatican, was enlightening on many aspects of Catholicism in the United States. Richard Harfmann helped with biblical research and at most of the libraries listed above. He also oversaw the effort to order literally hundreds of microfilms. In that regard, we would like to extend special thanks to the librarians at

Onondaga Community College, the New York State College at Morrisville, and the Onondaga County Public Library for working to keep the microfilms coming.

On the home front, Edward and Anne Brinkley of Laguna Nigel, California, offered wise counsel and support throughout the work on this book. In addition, Andrew Travers of the Theodore Roosevelt Center at Tulane University contributed a great deal of assistance and good cheer. Warren and Ruth Fenster of Porter, New York, reviewed the manuscript and offered insightful criticism along the way, and, finally, there is Neddy.

Notes

Preface

1. Frances Chamberlain, "Was There a Saint Born in Waterbury?," *The New York Times*, Sept. 13, 1998, sect. 14CN, p. 15.

1. A Friend of the Family

1. Delores Ann Liptak, "European Immigrants and the Catholic Church in Connecticut, 1870–1920" (Ph.D. diss., University of Connecticut, 1979), p. 6.
2. "The Irish Situation," *North American Review*, July 1848, pp. 141–42.
3. William Forbes Adams, *Ireland and Irish Emigration to the New World* (New York: Russell & Russell, 1932), p. 336.
4. Paul R. Keroack, "Michael Downes and His Descendants," typescript (1995), New Haven Colony Historical Society, New Haven, Conn., p. 1.
5. Ibid.
6. Adams, *Ireland and Irish Emigration*, p. 341.
7. *Benham's New Haven Directory and Annual Advertiser for 1868–9,*

no. 29 (New Haven: J. B. Benham, 1868), unnumbered advertising page.

8. *Catalogue of St. Charles College* (Baltimore: John Murphy & Co., 1880), p. 3.

9. Ibid., p. 8.

10. *Yale University Obituary Record of Graduates Deceased During the Year Ending July 1, 1922* (New Haven: Yale University, 1922), p. 565.

11. Rev. Joseph Gordian Daley, "The Personality of Fr. McGivney," *The Columbiad* 7, no. 6 (June 1900), p. 2.

12. Keroack, "Michael Downes and His Descendants," p. 1.

13. "Another Storm," *New Haven Palladium*, Feb. 6, 1882, p. 4.

14. "The Walks Neglected," *New Haven Palladium*, Feb. 6, 1882, p. 4.

15. New Haven Probate records, Feb. 6, 1882, vol. 168, p. 148, in Connecticut State Library, Hartford.

2. An American Child

1. Jean-Paul Gelinas, *The True Knight of Columbus* (n.p.: Pennsylvania State Council, Knights of Columbus, 1961), p. 44.

2. "K. of C. Memorial Day," *Waterbury Democrat*, June 9, 1900, p. 1.

3. Gelinas, *True Knight of Columbus,* p. 44.

4. "K. of C. Memorial Day," p. 1.

5. Thomas S. Duggan, *The Catholic Church in Connecticut* (New York: States History Co., 1930), p. 408.

6. *The Story of 100 Years* (Waterbury, Conn.: Immaculate Conception Parish, 1947), p. 31.

7. The number of children is usually counted as thirteen, but according to research by the Reverend Arthur J. Riley, Ph.D., in the early 1950s, only twelve could be traced in city and church records. Riley notes, Knights of Columbus Archives, New Haven, Conn., KC-4-1-079, pp. 3–5.

8. Rev. Joseph Gordian Daley, "The Personality of Fr. Mc-Givney," *The Columbiad* 7, no. 6 (June 1900).

9. "Death's Summons," *Providence Visitor*, June 19, 1886, in University of Notre Dame Archives, Notre Dame, Ind., CDPV/2.16.

10. *The Story of 100 Years*, p. 32.

11. "In Memoriam," *Providence Visitor*, June 19, 1886, in University of Notre Dame Archives, CDPV/2.16.

12. "Founder of the Order," *Waterbury Democrat*, June 8, 1901, p. 1.

13. Daley, "The Personality of Fr. McGivney."

3. The Priesthood

1. John Tracy Ellis, *The Life of James Cardinal Gibbons* (Milwaukee: Bruce, 1952), 1:443.

2. James Gibbons, *The Ambassador of Christ* (Baltimore: J. Murphy & Co., 1896), p. 15.

3. Jacques Millet, *Jesus Living in the Priest*, trans. Rev. Thomas Byrne (New York: Benziger, 1901), p. 474.

4. Gibbons, *Ambassador of Christ*, p. 215.

5. Millet, *Jesus Living in the Priest*, p. 14.

6. Ibid., pp. 26–27.

7. James Hennessy, *American Catholics* (New York: Oxford University Press, 1981), p. 163.

8. Anthony Viéban, "The Ecclesiastical Seminary," *The Catholic Encyclopedia* (New York: Gilmary, 1912); John Tracy Ellis, "The Formation of the American Priest: An Historical Perspective," in *The Catholic Priest in the United States*, ed. John Ellis Tracy (Collegeville, Minn.: St. John's University Press, 1971), p. 17.

9. Ellis, "Formation of the American Priest," pp. 41–49.

10. Robert F. Hueston, *The Catholic Press and Nativism* (New York: Arno, 1981), pp. 70–78.

11. Hennessy, *American Catholics*, pp. 124–25.
12. "Bishop Thomas F. Hendricken and the Cathedral," *The Providence Visitor*, 1997.
13. John K. Sharp, *History of the Diocese of Brooklyn* (New York: Fordham University Press, 1954), 1:252.
14. Gibbons, *Ambassador of Christ*, p. 19.
15. Pierre Veuillot, *The Catholic Priesthood According to the Teachings of the Church* (Westminster, Md.: Newman Press, 1958), pp. 234–37.

4. A Start in Seminary

1. "Il y a 100 ans," *L'Annuaire du séminaire de Saint-Hyacinthe* (St. Hyacinthe, Quebec: Seminary, 1968), p. 88; typescript translation in Knights of Columbus Archives, New Haven, Conn., KC-1-2-032.
2. Walter D. Wagoner, *The Seminary, Protestant and Catholic* (New York: Sheed & Ward, 1966), p. 197.
3. "Bishop Thomas F. Hendricken and the French Canadians," *The Providence Visitor*, 1997.
4. Charles Philippe Choquette, "Saint Hyacinthe," *The Catholic Encyclopedia* (New York: Gilmary, 1912), 13:352.
5. "Il y a 100 ans," p. 89.
6. Alfred LaLime, "The Founder of the Knights of Columbus, Student at St. Hyacinthe," manuscript (1968), p. 3, n. 3, K of C Archives.
7. Anthony Viéban, "Seminary," *The Catholic Encyclopedia* 13:702.
8. Very Rev. Francis X. Desmond, letter to Rev. Arthur J. Riley, February 1, 1950, K of C Archives, KC-1-2-33, Box 38.
9. Advertisement, "Seminary of Our Lady of Angels," *Connecticut Catholic*, June 3, 1876, p. 56.
10. *That All May Know Thee, 1856–1956: Niagaran Centennial Edition* (Lewiston, N.Y.: Niagara University, 1956), p. 28.
11. *History of the Seminary of Our Lady of Angels* (Buffalo: Matthews-Northrup Works, 1906), p. 178.

12. *Catalogue of the Officers and Students of the Seminary of Our Lady of Angels, 1871–72* (n.p.: Niagarensis, 1871).

13. "Death of Dr. James P. Splain," *New Haven Morning Journal and Courier,* Mar. 12, 1883, p. 2.

14. *Index Niagarensis,* various issues, 1871–72.

15. *History of the Seminary of Our Lady of Angels,* p. 330.

16. Ibid., p. 324.

17. "Base Ball," *Index Niagarensis,* June 1, 1871.

18. Desmond, to Riley, February 1, 1950.

19. "Base Ball," *Index Niagarensis,* June 1, 1872, p. 139.

20. "Father Rice's Birthday," *Index Niagarensis,* June 15, 1872, p. 149.

21. *History of the Seminary of Our Lady of Angels,* p. 324.

22. "The Past Year," *Index Niagarensis,* June 26, 1872, p. 155.

23. J. P. McKey, *History of Niagara University* (Niagara University, N.Y.: Niagara University, 1931), p. 251.

24. "K. of C. Memorial Day," Waterbury *Democrat,* June 9, 1900, p. 1.

25. Student account ledger, Our Lady of Angels Seminary, K of C Archives.

26. "Death's Summons," *Providence Visitor,* June 19, 1886, p. 1.

27. Rev. Joseph Gordian Daley, "The Personality of Fr. Mc-Givney," *The Columbiad* 7, no. 6 (June 1900).

28. Garry Wills, *Why I Am a Catholic* (Boston: Houghton Mifflin, 2002), p. 20.

5. In the City of New Haven

1. "Rev. Father Lawlor Dead," *New Haven Sunday Union,* Mar. 21, 1886, p. 1.

2. Rev. Joseph Gordian Daley, "The Personality of Fr. Mc-Givney," *The Columbiad* 7, no. 6 (June 1900).

3. *Catholic University Bulletin,* Dec. 1918, p. 150, quoted in John Tracy Ellis, *The Life of James Cardinal Gibbons* (Milwaukee: Bruce, 1952), 1:29.

4. Jean-Paul Gelinas, *The True Knight of Columbus* (n.p.: Pennsylvania State Council, Knights of Columbus, 1961), p. 50.

5. James Cardinal Gibbons, *A Retrospective of Fifty Years* (Baltimore: John Murphy Co., 1916), pp. 12–13.

6. "Personal," *New Haven Morning Journal and Courier*, Jan. 8, 1878, p. 2.

7. "Death of P.A. Murphy," *Connecticut Catholic*, May 24, 1879, p. 1.

8. Untitled entry, *New Haven Evening Register*, Jan. 21, 1878, p. 4.

9. "Death of Dr. Carmody," *New Haven Evening Register*, Apr. 23, 1883, p. 1.

10. *Reminiscences of Dr. Edwin Harwood, D.D.* (New York: Trinity Press, 1903), pp. 12–13; Stewart Means, *In Memoriam Edwin Harwood* (New Haven, 1902), pp. 16–17.

11. Waleska B. Evans, *A Cornerstone of 1871 Focuses a Bustling New Haven* (New Haven: New Haven Historical Society, 1960), p. 7.

12. "The Telephone," *New Haven Palladium*, Feb. 15, 1878, p. 4.

13. "St. Joseph's Cathedral," *New Haven Morning Journal and Courier*, Feb. 11, 1878, p. 2.

14. "Mourning for Pope Pius IX," *New Haven Evening Register*, Feb. 18, 1878, p. 4.

15. U.S. Census, 1880, New Haven, Conn., roll 79–105.

16. "The Catholic Church: Its Practice," *New Haven Morning Journal and Courier*, Mar. 16, 1878, p. 1.

6. In Charge

1. Thomas F. Clark, quoted in Jean-Paul Gelinas, *The True Knight of Columbus* (n.p.: Pennsylvania State Council, Knights of Columbus, 1961), p. 57. All Thomas Clark quotations in this passage are from this source.

2. Rev. Joseph Gordian Daley, "The Personality of Fr. McGivney," *The Columbiad* 7, no. 6 (June 1900).

3. Ibid.

4. W. J. Slocum, "Father Slocum's Address," *Souvenir Twentieth Anniversary of Sheridan Council* (Waterbury, Conn.: 1905), p. 29.

5. "The Fair of St. John's Church," *New Haven Evening Register*, Feb. 25, 1878, p. 4.

6. "St. Patrick's Day," *New Haven Evening Register*, Mar. 18, 1878, p. 4.

7. "Roman Catholic Burial Association," *New Haven Evening Register*, May 27, 1878, p. 4; "New Haven," *Connecticut Catholic*, June 8, 1878, p. 5.

8. "New Haven," *Connecticut Catholic*, June 8, 1878, p. 5.

9. U.S. Census, 1870 and 1880, New Haven, Conn., Ward 3, various pages.

10. *Semi-Centennial Anniversary of Father Mathew's Visit to New Haven, Conn.* (New Haven, 1899), pp. 22, 28.

11. "New Haven," *Connecticut Catholic*, June 29, 1878, p. 5.

12. "Board of Health," *New Haven Palladium*, July 3, 1878, p. 4.

13. "Up in the Nineties," *New Haven Evening Register*, July 18, 1878, p. 1.

14. "New Haven," *Connecticut Catholic*, July 20, 1878, p. 2.

15. "Personal," *New Haven Morning Journal and Courier*, July 11, 1878, p. 2.

16. "Father Carmody's Departure," *New Haven Morning Journal and Courier*, July 12, 1878, p. 4; "Father Carmody," *New Haven Morning Journal and Courier*, July 15, 1878, p. 4; "Waiting on the Bishop," *New Haven Evening Register*, July 16, 1878, p. 1.

17. Michael McGivney, letter to Alphonse Magnien, October 21, 1878, Knights of Columbus Archives, New Haven, Conn.

18. Untitled article, *New Haven Palladium*, Aug. 3, 1878, p. 4; "A Sad Case of Insanity," *New Haven Morning Journal and Courier*, Aug. 3, 1878, p. 4.

19. "Catholic Picnics," *Connecticut Catholic*, June 29, 1878, p. 1.

20. "New Haven," *Connecticut Catholic*, Aug. 10, 1878, p. 2; "New Haven," *Connecticut Catholic*, Aug. 17, 1878, p. 2; *New Haven Morning Journal and Courier*, Aug. 8, 1878, p. 4.

7. A Church Fair

1. Thomas Walsh, letter to New Haven pastors, published in *Connecticut Catholic*, Oct. 26, 1878, p. 2.

2. Henrietta Frances Dana, *Hillhouse Avenue from 1809 to 1900* (New Haven: Tuttle, Moorehouse & Taylor, 1900), pp. 10–11.

3. Dick Bissell, "To Talk of Many Things," in *In the Early Eighties and Since with Yale '83* (privately printed, 1923), p. 25; Manuscripts and Archives, Yale University.

4. "New Haven," *Connecticut Catholic*, Sept. 6, 1879, p. 2.

5. "Cornelius T. Driscoll," *New Haven Union,* Souvenir section, Oct. 11, 1892, in Knights of Columbus Archives, New Haven, Conn., KC-1-4 (Cornelius Driscoll); Arthur J. Riley, interview notes with Miss Jane Curran, June 16, 1950, K of C Archives, KC-4-1-074; *Yale Obituary Record, 1930–34* (New Haven: Yale University, 1934), p. 12.

6. "Catholic T.A. Unions," *New Haven Evening Register*, Sept. 9, 1879, p. 4.

7. "Bishop McMahon," *Connecticut Catholic*, Jan. 31, 1879, p. 3.

8. "Rev. P.A. Murphy," *New Haven Evening Register,* May 19, 1879, p. 4; "New Haven," *Connecticut Catholic,* Feb. 8, 1879, p. 3.

9. "Various Matters," *New Haven Evening Register*, Feb. 19, 1879, p. 2.

10. "New Haven," *Connecticut Catholic,* Aug. 23, 1879, p. 3.

11. "New Haven," *Connecticut Catholic*, Mar. 8, 1879, p. 2.

12. "New Haven, *Connecticut Catholic*, Mar. 22, 1879, p. 2.

13. "Success of the Telephone," *New Haven Evening Register*, Feb. 1, 1879, p. 4; "How the City Is Lighted," *New Haven Evening Register*, Jan. 3, 1879, p. 4; "A Trial of the Electric Light," *New Haven Evening Register*, Feb. 1, 1879, p. 4.

14. "Death of Rev. P.A. Murphy," *New Haven Morning Journal and Courier*, May 20, 1879, p. 2.

15. "Serious Illness of P.A. Murphy," *New Haven Morning Journal and Courier*, May 19, 1879, p. 2.

16. "An Unprofitable Church," *The New York Times*, July 28, 1879, p. 1.
17. "A Church's Finances," *New Haven Morning Journal and Courier*, July 29, 1879, p. 4.
18. "Various Frailties," *New Haven Union*, Aug. 5, 1879, p. 4.
19. "Various Matters," *New Haven Evening Register*, July 16, 1879, p. 4; "An Interesting Occasion," *New Haven Evening Register*, Aug. 1, 1879, p. 4; "A Literary Entertainment," *New Haven Evening Register*, Aug. 15, 1879, p. 4.
20. Advertisement, *New Haven Evening Register*, Nov. 5, 1879, p. 4.
21. "The Catholic Parishes," *New Haven Evening Register*, Sept. 25, 1879, p. 4.

8. Modern Men

1. James T. Mullen biographical timeline, Knights of Columbus Archives, New Haven, Conn., KC-4-1; U.S. Census, 1880, New Haven, Conn., roll T9-109.
2. Felix John Vondracek, "The Rise of Fraternal Organizations in the United States, 1868–1900," *Social Science*, Winter 1971, pp. 27–28.
3. Robert Leeney, "Supreme Knight James T. Mullen," *Columbia*, July 1991, p. 17; "Elections of Officers," *New Haven Palladium*, Feb. 7, 1878, p. 4.
4. "The Old Trouble Again," *New Haven Union*, July 12, 1883, p. 4.
5. "Bernhardt's Funeral," *New Haven Evening Register*, July 12, 1883, p. 4.
6. Ibid.
7. "Pyke O'Callaghan," *New Haven Evening Register*, Mar. 18, 1880, p. 4.
8. "New Haven," *Connecticut Catholic*, Mar. 27, 1880, p. 2.
9. "New Haven," *Connecticut Catholic*, May 22, 1880, p. 2.
10. "New Haven," *Connecticut Catholic*, Oct. 2, 1880, p. 3.
11. "New Haven," *Connecticut Catholic*, Feb. 18, 1882, p. 2.

12. Adele Francis Gorman, "Evolution of Catholic Lay Leadership," *Historical Records and Studies* 50 (1964), p. 130.

13. Michael J. McGivney, preprinted circular letter, Apr. 1882, K of C Archives.

9. McGivney's Solution

1. William Geary and Cornelius Driscoll, "History of the Founding of the Knights of Columbus," manuscript (1923), Knights of Columbus Archives, New Haven, Conn., K-1-1-103, Box 33, Geary Papers. McGivney was actually twenty-nine at the time.

2. Shepard B. Clough, *A Century of American Life Insurance* (New York: Columbia University Press, 1946), p. 46.

3. Robert Whaples and David Buffum, "Fraternalism, Paternalism, the Family and the Market: Insurance a Century Ago," *Social Science History* 15, no. 1 (Spring 1991), p. 103.

4. "New Haven," *Connecticut Catholic,* Jan. 7, 1882, p. 3.

5. Whaples and Buffum, "Fraternalism, Paternalism, the Family and the Market," p. 103.

6. Delores Liptak, *Hartford's Catholic Legacy: Leadership* (Hartford: Archdiocese of Hartford, 1999), p. 151.

7. John K. Sharp, *History of the Diocese of Brooklyn* (New York: Fordham University Press, 1954), 2:237.

8. Knights of Columbus Supreme Council minutes, Feb. 2, 1882, typescript copy, K of C Archives, KC-7-1-055, Box 28.

9. Knights of Columbus minutes, Feb. 2, 1882, typescript copy, K of C Archives, KC-7-1-055, Box 28.

10. "Christopher Columbus," *Connecticut Catholic,* May 25, 1878, p. 1.

11. "James T. Mullen," K of C Archives, KC-1-121, Box 34 (Daniel Colwell Papers).

12. Ibid.

13. Knights of Columbus minutes, Feb. 2, 1882, original copybook, K of C Archives, KC-1-1.

14. Michael McGivney, letter to Martin I.J. Griffin, Feb. 12, 1883, K of C Archives.
15. Geary and Driscoll, "History of the Founding."
16. "Lodge and Society," *New Haven Morning Journal and Courier*, Feb. 8, 1882, p. 3.
17. "The Catholic Foresters," *New Haven Evening Register*, Feb. 8, 1882, p. 4.
18. "Various Matters," *New Haven Evening Register*, Mar. 3, 1882, p. 4.
19. Knights of Columbus minutes, Mar. 1, 1882, typescript copy, K of C Archives, KC-7-1-055, Box 28.
20. Michael J. McGivney, preprinted circular letter, Apr. 1882, K of C Archives.
21. Whaples and Buffum, "Fraternalism, Paternalism, the Family and the Market," p. 102.

10. A Bleak Night in Ansonia

1. "Smith Is Bound Over," *New Haven Evening Register*, Dec. 29, 1880, p. 1.
2. "How Smith Took It," *New Haven Evening Register*, Apr. 19, 1881, p. 1.
3. "A Murderer's Fortune," *New Haven Evening Register*, Mar. 2, 1882, p. 1.
4. "Practically Doomed," *New Haven Palladium*, Mar. 16, 1882, p. 4.
5. " 'Chip' Reconciled," *New Haven Union*, Aug. 1, 1882, p. 1.
6. William Geary and Cornelius Driscoll, "History of the Founding of the Knights of Columbus," manuscript (1923), Knights of Columbus Archives, New Haven, Conn., K-1-1-103, Box 33, Geary Papers.
7. "New Haven," *Connecticut Catholic*, Apr. 22, 1882, p. 2.
8. Advertisement, "General Tom Thumb and Wife," *New Haven Palladium*, May 17, 1882, p. 1; D. H. Buel, *Penikeese; or*

Cuisine and Cupid (New York: William A. Pond, 1882), Manuscripts and Archives, Yale University.

9. "Various Matters," *New Haven Evening Register*, May 2, 1882, p. 4.

10. "Various Matters," *New Haven Evening Register*, June 6, 1882, p. 4.

11. Michael McGivney, letter to Michael Edmonds, June 7, 1882, K of C Archives, New Haven, Conn.

12. "The Knights of Columbus," *New Haven Evening Register*, June 16, 1882, p. 4.

13. "New Haven," *Connecticut Catholic*, Aug. 12, 1882, p. 2.

14. "Chip Smith's Death," *New Haven Evening Register*, Aug. 30, 1882, p. 1.

15. "New Haven," *Connecticut Catholic*, Sept. 2, 1882, p. 2.

16. "High Mass Last Sunday," *New Haven Palladium*, Aug. 28, 1882, p. 1.

17. " 'Chip' Smith," *New Haven Union*, Aug. 29, 1882, p. 1.

18. "Chip Smith Dies Bravely," *New Haven Union*, Sept. 1, 1882, p. 1.

19. "Gallows and Man Ready," *New Haven Union*, Aug. 31, 1882, p. 1.

11. Inertia in a Hurry

1. William Geary and Cornelius Driscoll, "History of the Founding of the Knights of Columbus," Manuscript (1923), Knights of Columbus Archives, New Haven, Conn., K-1-1-103, Box 33, Geary Papers.

2. "The Irish Sufferers," *New Haven Evening Register*, Jan. 22, 1880, p. 2.

3. Jane Curran, interview with Rev. Arthur Riley, June 16, 1950, transcript, K of C Archives, KC-4-1-074.

4. Geary and Driscoll, "History of the Founding."

5. Ibid.

6. Patrick W. Carey, *The Roman Catholics* (Westport, Conn.: Greenwood, 1993), p. 31.

7. Roger Finke and Rodney Stark, *The Churching of America, 1776–1990* (New Brunswick, N.J.: Rutgers University Press, 1992), p. 113.

8. "The Roman Catholic Question, II," *The International Review* 8 (March 1880), p. 300.

9. George E. Ellis, "The Roman Church and American Institutions," *Unitarian Review* 13, no. 5 (May 1880), p. 400.

10. Geary and Driscoll, "History of the Founding."

11. "New Haven," *Connecticut Catholic*, July 8, 1882, p. 2; "New Haven," *Connecticut Catholic*, Mar. 10, 1883, p. 2.

12. "Children of Neglect," *New Haven Evening Register*, Oct. 28, 1882, p. 1.

13. "Death of James P. Splain," *New Haven Morning Journal and Courier*, Mar. 12, 1883, p. 2; "Funeral of James P. Splain," *New Haven Morning Journal and Courier*, Mar. 13, 1883, p. 2.

14. "Life in Connecticut," *New Haven Evening Register*, Mar. 6, 1883, p. 4.

15. "Sudden Death," *New Haven Morning Journal and Courier*, Jan. 19, 1883, p. 2.

16. "Death from Starvation," *New Haven Evening Register*, Feb. 8, 1883, p. 4.

12. Faith in Meriden

1. George O'Connor, "A History of Silver City Council No. 2," Jan. 15, 1895, manuscript, Knights of Columbus Archives, New Haven, Conn., SLC-008-5-00002-002.

2. McGivney quoted ibid.

3. Ibid.

4. McGivney quoted ibid.

5. "The Late Rev. Hugh Carmody," *New Haven Morning Journal and Courier*, Apr. 24, 1883, p. 4.

6. "Rev. Dr. Hugh Carmody D.D.," *New Haven Union*, Apr. 23, 1883, p. 1.

7. "Death of Dr. Carmody," *New Haven Evening Register*, Apr. 23, 1883, p. 1.

8. "Meriden," *Connecticut Catholic*, Apr. 28, 1883, p. 2.

9. O'Connor, "A History of Silver City Council No. 2."

10. U.S. Census, 1880, New Haven, Conn., roll T9-106; Everett G. Hill, *A Modern History of New Haven and Eastern New Haven County* (New York: S.J. Clarke, 1918), 1:294; "Parishes," French-Canadian Genealogical Society of Connecticut Archives, Tolland, Conn.

11. O'Connor, "A History of Silver City Council No. 2."

12. Ibid.

13. A Stern Voice

1. The *New London Day* piece of March 26, 1883, was reprinted in "Occasioning Gossip," *New Haven Evening Register*, Mar. 27, 1883, p. 4.

2. Everett G. Hill, *A Modern History of New Haven and Eastern New Haven County* (New York: S. J. Clarke, 1918), 1:122; "Annual Meeting of Trinity Church," *New Haven Morning Journal and Courier*, Apr. 14, 1884, p. 2.

3. U.S. Census, 1880, Assiniboine, Chouteau, Mont., roll 79-742.

4. "Funeral of Miss Harwood," *Queens County Sentinel*, Oct. 22, 1885, p. 4; "Death of Miss Alida Van S. Harwood," *New Haven Morning Journal and Courier*, Oct. 10, 1885, p. 2.

5. "Various Matters," *New Haven Evening Register*, Apr. 9, 1883, p. 2.

6. "Dr. Harwood to Resign," *New Haven Evening Register*, Apr. 25, 1883, p. 1.

7. "Personal," *New Haven Morning Journal and Courier*, July 19, 1883, p. 4; "Personal," *New Haven Evening Register*, July 31, 1883, p. 1.

8. Rev. Joseph Gordian Daley, "The Personality of Fr. Mc-Givney," *The Columbiad* 7, no. 6 (June 1900).

9. *Yale University Class of 1883 Biographical Record*, Manuscripts and Archives, Yale University.

10. "Large Excursion to Coney Island," *New Haven Evening Register*, Aug. 1, 1883, p. 4.

11. "Denounced in Church," *New Haven Evening Register*, Sept. 3, 1883, p. 1.

12. "Catholic Foresters," *New Haven Evening Register*, Sept. 14, 1883, p. 4; "Personal," *New Haven Morning Journal and Courier*, Oct. 20, 1883, p. 2.

13. "Services at St. Mary's Church," *New Haven Morning Journal and Courier*, Oct. 8, 1883, p. 2.

14. "Penikeese," *New Haven Morning Journal and Courier*, Jan. 29, 1884, p. 2.

15. "Musical," *New Haven Morning Journal and Courier*, Mar. 12, 1884, p. 2.

16. "Choirs and Singing," *New Haven Morning Journal and Courier*, May 5, 1884, p. 2.

17. "Various Matters," *New Haven Morning Journal and Courier*, Dec. 28, 1883, p. 2.

18. "A Choir Protected from Statues," *New Haven Morning Journal and Courier*, May 5, 1884, p. 4.

19. "Of Interest to Catholics," *New Haven Union*, May 12, 1884, p. 1.

20. "Supreme Council," *New Haven Morning Journal and Courier*, May 7, 1884, p. 2.

21. "Political Notes," *New Haven Morning News*, Nov. 3, 1884, p. 3.

22. "'Rum, Romanism and Rebellion,'" *New Haven Evening Register*, Nov. 3, 1884, p. 1.

23. "An Affecting Scene," *New Haven Evening Register*, Nov. 10, 1884, p. 4.

14. Talk of the Town

1. "Funeral of Miss Harwood," *Queens County Sentinel*, Oct. 22, 1885, p. 4.
2. "Thomaston," *Connecticut Catholic*, Mar. 14, 1885, p. 5.
3. "Secret Societies—Knights of Columbus," *Connecticut Catholic*, May 16, 1885, p. 4.
4. John D. Barrett, *A Comparative Study of the Councils of Baltimore and the Code of Canon Law* (Washington, D.C.: Catholic University Press, 1932), pp. 16–18.
5. Ibid., pp. 115–16.
6. "Secret Societies," *Connecticut Catholic*, May 16, 1885, p. 4.
7. Michael McGivney, "Knights of Columbus," *Connecticut Catholic*, May 30, 1885, p. 4.
8. Michael J. McGivney, preprinted circular letter, Apr. 1882, Knights of Columbus Archives, New Haven, Conn.
9. "The Harwood Sensation," *New Haven Evening Register*, Oct. 1, 1885, p. 1; "Wedding Him She Loved," *New Haven Morning News*, Oct. 1, 1885, p. 1.
10. "Rev. Dr. Harwood's Daughter," *New Haven Evening Register*, Oct. 15, 1885, p. 1.
11. "The Last Ceremonies," *New Haven Evening Register*, Oct. 19, 1885, p. 1.
12. "Funeral of Miss Harwood," p. 4.
13. Ibid.
14. "The Last Ceremonies," *New Haven Evening Register*, Oct. 19, 1885, p. 1.
15. "Beginning to Arrive," *New Haven Evening Register*, Oct. 19, 1885, p. 1.

15. A Priest's Life

1. Untitled article, *Waterbury Daily American*, Jan. 5, 1886.
2. "Rev. P. P. Lawlor," *Connecticut Catholic,* Mar. 27, 1886, p. 7; "Rev. Father Lawlor Dead," *New Haven Sunday Union*, Mar. 21, 1886, p. 1.
3. "Various Matters," *New Haven Morning Journal and Courier*, Jan. 14, 1878, p. 2; "Fath. Lawlor's Funeral," *New Haven Evening Register*, Mar. 22, 1886, p. 1.
4. "Rev. James C. O'Brien," *Catholic Transcript*, Jan. 19, 1928; untitled column, New Haven *Morning Journal and Courier*, Apr. 25, 1878, p. 3.
5. Untitled article, *Waterbury Daily American*, Nov. 26, 1886.
6. "Thomaston," *Connecticut Catholic*, Apr. 3, 1886, p. 1.
7. Untitled article, *Waterbury Daily American*, Mar. 30, 1887.
8. "Thomaston," *Connecticut Catholic*, Aug. 4, 1888, p. 5.
9. "Thomaston," *Connecticut Catholic*, Apr. 24, 1886, p. 1.
10. Untitled article, *Waterbury Daily American*, Nov. 20, 1886.
11. "Thomaston," *Connecticut Catholic*, Dec. 5, 1887, p. 5.
12. Ibid.
13. "They Bid Farewell to School," *Waterbury Democrat*, Apr. 17, 1888, p. 4.
14. Rev. Joseph Gordian Daley, "The Personality of Fr. McGivney," *The Columbiad* 7, no. 6 (June 1900), p. 2.
15. "Mrs. Mary McGivney," *Waterbury Evening Democrat*, Dec. 10, 1888, p. 4.
16. "The Bazar of the K. of C.," *Connecticut Catholic*, Feb. 11, 1888, p. 5.
17. "K. of C. in Rhode Island," *Connecticut Catholic*, Apr. 6, 1889, p. 5.
18. Untitled article, *Waterbury Republican*, July 17, 1890; "Obituary," *Waterbury Republican*, Aug. 15, 1890.
19. Untitled article, *Waterbury Daily American*, June 2, 1888.

Epilogue

1. "Death of Father McGivney," *Waterbury Evening Democrat,* Aug. 14, 1890.
2. "Knights of Columbus," *Connecticut Catholic,* July 4, 1891, p. 8.
3. Michael J. McGivney, Last Will and Testament, Aug. 9, 1890, Knights of Columbus Archives, New Haven, Conn., KC-1-2-039.
4. Paul R. Keroack, "Michael Downes and His Descendants," typescript (1995), New Haven Colony Historical Society, New Haven, Conn., pp. 11–12.
5. *Yale University Obituary Record of Graduates Deceased During the Year Ending July 1, 1922* (New Haven: Yale University, 1922), p. 565.
6. *Yale University Obituary Record of Graduates Deceased During the Years 1921–25* (New Haven: Yale University, 1925), p. 736.
7. "Dr. Stephen Maher, Tuberculosis Foe," *The New York Times,* June 7, 1939, p. 29; *Yale University Obituary Record of Graduates Deceased During the Years 1938–40* (New Haven: Yale University, 1940), pp. 248–49.

Selected Bibliography

Adams, William Forbes. *Ireland and Irish Emigration to the New World*. New York: Russell & Russell, 1932.

Anderson, Floyd. *Father Baker*. Milwaukee: Bruce, 1960.

Barrett, John D. *A Comparative Study of the Councils of Baltimore and the Code of Canon Law*. Washington, D.C.: Catholic University Press, 1932.

Billington, Ray Allen. *The Protestant Crusade, 1800–1860: A Study of the Origins of American Nativism*. New York: Rinehart, 1938.

Bland, Joan. *Hibernian Crusade: The Story of the Catholic Total Abstinence Union of America*. Washington, D.C.: Catholic University of America Press, 1951.

Carnes, Mark C. *Secret Ritual and Manhood in Victorian America*. New Haven: Yale University Press, 1989.

Clawson, Mary Ann. *Constructing Brotherhood, Class, Gender and Fraternalism*. Princeton, N.J.: Princeton University Press, 1989.

Cross, Robert. *The Emergence of Liberal Catholicism in America*. Cambridge, Mass.: Harvard University Press, 1958.

Dolan, Jay P. *The American Catholic Experience*. Garden City, N.Y.: Doubleday, 1985.

————. *Immigrant Church: New York's Irish and German Catholics*. Baltimore: Johns Hopkins University Press, 1975.

Duggan, Thomas C. *The Catholic Church in Connecticut*. New York: States History Co., 1930.

Ellis, John Tracy. *The Life of James Cardinal Gibbons*. Milwaukee: Bruce, 1952.

Fell, Marie Lennore. *The Foundations of Nativism in American Textbooks, 1963–1860*. Washington, D.C.: Catholic University of America Press, 1941.

Fitton, James. *Sketches of the Establishment of the Church in New England*. Boston: P. Donahoe, 1872.

Gibbons, James Cardinal. *The Ambassador of Christ*. Baltimore: J. Murphy & Co., 1896.

———. *A Retrospective of Fifty Years*. Baltimore: John Murphy & Co., 1916.

Hogan, Neil. *Cry of the Famishing*. East Haven, Conn.: Connecticut Irish-American Historical Society, 1998.

Kauffman, Christopher J. *Faith and Fraternalism: The History of the Knights of Columbus, 1882–1982*. New York: Harper & Row, 1982.

Keatinge, James. *The Priest: His Character and Work*. London: Kegan Paul, Trench, Trubney, 1935.

Keroack, Paul R. "Michael Downes and His Descendants." Typescript (1995). New Haven Colony Historical Society, New Haven, Conn.

Liptak, Delores Ann. "European Immigrants and the Catholic Church in Connecticut, 1870–1920." Ph.D. diss., University of Connecticut, 1979.

———. *Hartford's Catholic Legacy: Leadership*. Hartford: Archdiocese of Hartford, 1999.

MacDonald, Fergus. *The Catholic Church and the Secret Societies in the United States*. New York: U.S. Catholic Historical Society, 1946.

Marty, Martin E. *Pilgrims in Their Own Land: 500 Years of Religion in America*. Boston: Little, Brown, 1984.

———. *Righteous Empire: The Protestant Experience in America*. New York: Dial Press, 1970.

SELECTED BIBLIOGRAPHY 233

McAvoy, Thomas T. "The Irish Clergyman in the United States," *American Catholic Historical Society Records* 75, no. 1 (Mar. 1964).

Millet, Jacques. *Jesus Living in the Priest*. Translated by Thomas Byrne. New York: Benziger, 1901.

Myers, Gustavus. *History of Bigotry in the United States*. New York: Random House, 1943.

Noonan, Carroll J. *Nativism in Connecticut*. Washington, D.C.: Catholic University of America Press, 1938.

O'Donnell, James H. *History of the Diocese of Hartford*. Boston: D.H. Hurd, 1900.

Sharp, John K. *History of the Diocese of Brooklyn*. 2 vols. New York: Fordham University Press, 1954.

Veuillot, Pierre. *The Catholic Priesthood According to the Teaching of the Church*. Westminster, Md.: Newman Press, 1958.

Willging, Eugene. *Catholic Serials of the Nineteenth Century in the United States*. Washington, D.C.: Catholic University of America Press, 1959.

Index